Parenting Toddlers

How You Can Use Positive Discipline to Raise Kids Who Will Have High Self-Esteem, Including Tips for Sleep Training, Handing Tantrums and a Guide to Potty Training

© Copyright 2020

The contents of this book may not be reproduced, duplicated or transmitted without direct written permission from the author.

Under no circumstances will any legal responsibility or blame be held against the publisher for any reparation, damages, or monetary loss due to the information herein, either directly or indirectly.

Legal Notice:

This book is copyright protected. This is only for personal use. You cannot amend, distribute, sell, use, quote or paraphrase any part or the content within this book without the consent of the author.

Disclaimer Notice:

Please note the information contained within this document is for educational and entertainment purposes only. Every attempt has been made to provide accurate, up to date and reliable complete information. No warranties of any kind are expressed or implied. Readers acknowledge that the author is not engaging in the rendering of legal, financial, medical or professional advice. The content of this book has been derived from various sources. Please consult a licensed professional before attempting any techniques outlined in this book.

By reading this document, the reader agrees that under no circumstances is the author responsible for any losses, direct or indirect, which are incurred as a result of the use of information contained within this document, including, but not limited to, —errors, omissions, or inaccuracies.

Contents

PART 1: TODDLER PARENTING 1
INTRODUCTION 2
CHAPTER ONE: WHAT IT MEANS TO BE A TODDLER 4
    Major Toddler Milestones 5
    Common Toddler Troubles 7
CHAPTER TWO: WHAT IS POSITIVE DISCIPLINE? 10
    Meaning of Positive Discipline 11
    Benefits of Positive Discipline 12
    Principles of Positive Discipline 13
    A Simple Exercise in Positive Discipline 16
CHAPTER THREE: POSITIVE PARENTING STARTS AT HOME (AND WITH YOU) 19
    Tips to Get Started with Positive Parenting 19
    Positive Discipline Techniques 24
CHAPTER FOUR: SLEEP TRAINING FOR YOUR TODDLER 29
    How to Sleep Train Your Toddler 29
    Positive Parenting and Sleep Training 33
CHAPTER FIVE: POTTY TRAINING YOUR TODDLER 44
    How to Start Potty Training 44

Tips to Prepare Your Toddler for Potty Training 47
Tips to Get Started With Potty Training 49
Positive Parenting and Potty Training 51

CHAPTER SIX: DEALING WITH TANTRUMS AND MISBEHAVIOR 58
Why Do Toddlers Misbehave? 59
Dealing with Toddler Tantrums 62

CHAPTER SEVEN: ENCOURAGING CREATIVITY AND IMAGINATION 67

CHAPTER EIGHT: BUILDING SELF-ESTEEM AND CONFIDENCE 73
Tips to Build Self-Confidence 74
Tips to Build Self-Esteem 77

CHAPTER NINE: FORMING POSITIVE DAILY HABITS 80
Positive Discipline for a Peaceful Home 80
Chores for Toddlers 82
Creating a Routine 85

CHAPTER TEN: GROWING OUT OF TODDLERDOM 88

CONCLUSION 94

PART 2: POTTY TRAINING 96

INTRODUCTION 97

CHAPTER ONE: WHEN TO START POTTY-TRAINING 99
Toddler Development and Potty-Training 102
Signs That Your Toddler is Ready for Potty-Training 108

CHAPTER TWO: POTTY-TRAINING MYTHS AND MISCONCEPTIONS 11

CHAPTER THREE: DITCHING DIAPERS (WITHOUT THE DRAMA) ... 120
Choosing the Right Potty Goes a Long Way 121
Let's Get Rid of the Diapers 123
Some Do's and Don'ts 123
Some Techniques to Help Your Child Ditch their Diapers Without the Drama 127

CHAPTER FOUR: POTTY-POOPING PSYCHOLOGY AND MENTAL PREPAREDNESS 129
Mentally Preparing Your Child for Potty-Training 129

Why Your Child's Having a Hard Time Potty-Training 130
Psychological Effects of Botched Potty-Training 136
CHAPTER FIVE: USING THE POTTY FOR THE FIRST TIME 139
CHAPTER SIX: POTTY AND POOPING PROBLEMS 148
How You Can Solve Some of These Potty-Training Problems 154
CHAPTER SEVEN: NIGHTTIME POTTY TRAINING 157
Difference Between Daytime and Nighttime Potty-Training 157
When to Start Nighttime Potty-Training 158
How Long Does Nighttime Potty-Training Last? 160
Tips You Can Follow 160
CHAPTER EIGHT: POTTY TRAINING GIRLS VS. BOYS 166
Ten Gender-Specific Tips to Help Your Toddler 169
CHAPTER NINE: FORMING POTTY HABITS 176
CHAPTER TEN: FROM POTTY TO ADULT TOILET 184
The Right Age to Transition to the Toilet 186
Tips to Make the Transition Easier 187
CONCLUSION 190
RESOURCES 192

Part 1: Toddler Parenting

The Ultimate Guide to Using Positive Discipline to Raise Children with High Self-Esteem, Including Tips for Sleep Training, Handing Tantrums, and Potty Training

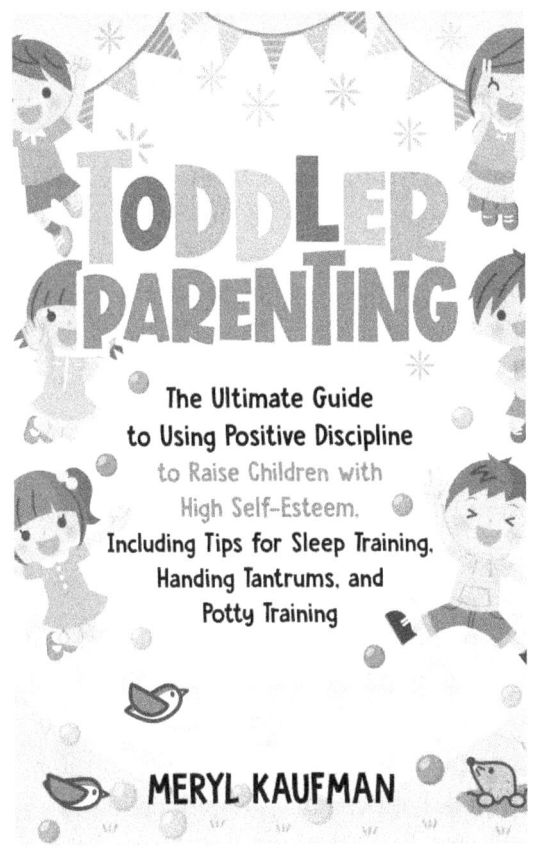

Introduction

Imagine a home with happy children who listen to their parents and don't misbehave. A home where no one must raise their voice, and everyone is happy. This book will give you all the information you need to turn this peaceful thought into reality. Raising a child isn't always easy, no matter how much love you have for your little one. No single approach would fit all children. Sometimes, you wish your toddler came with an instruction manual. Alas, this isn't the case.

Being a parent is perhaps one of the most memorable, dynamic, and exciting roles you will ever play. Parenting is rewarding and fruitful, but it can be difficult. Parents have no formal training before they are made responsible for dealing with kids. It can also be a little overwhelming and daunting. Even the best of us require some support. Well, you can rest easy because this book has all the information you need to understand about positive parenting to raise a well-adjusted, happy, and confident child.

In this book, you will learn about understanding your toddler's development, the meaning of positive discipline and its importance, and tips and suggestions to get started with positive parenting. You will also discover helpful and practical tips for potting training and sleep training for your toddler. Besides these things, you will learn about dealing with your toddler's tantrums, correcting any misbehavior, and helping your toddler form positive habits. When all the information in this book is implemented, it helps encourage your toddler's creativity and imagination and build self-esteem and confidence. Simple and practical tips for applying positive discipline once your toddler grows and enters the age of schooling are also included. This book includes all the information any parent would need to get started with positive parenting.

Once you follow the practical advice in this book, you will see a positive change in your toddler and the relationship you share. Taking care of children isn't just about looking after their basic needs of food, clothing, and shelter. An important aspect of parenthood and your duty as a parent is to equip your child with the skills he needs to survive in the real world. As with everything else, the sooner you start, the more effective and efficient are the results. A little love, patience, consistency, and effort are all you need to change your toddler's behavior.

Are you eager to learn more about all this? Do you want to discover the concepts of successfully parenting your toddler? If yes, let's get started without further ado!

Chapter One: What It Means To Be A Toddler

There are different terms used to describe children between the ages of birth to four years, such as infants, babies, newborns, and toddlers. These terms are often used synonymously, but there is a slight difference between each. Until the baby is two months old, he is called a newborn. The infant is a term used to refer to children until they are 12 months old. Baby is a term collectively used to refer to children who are or less than four years old. Therefore, it includes all the other terms, such as infants, toddlers, and newborns.

Who is a toddler? It turns out there isn't any official definition or an upper limit to the term toddler. Often, it's a term used to define children between the ages group of 12-36 months. The Centers use the same definition For Disease Control And Prevention. A toddler is a child who is learning to walk or toddles. This stage usually starts when a child is about 12 months old. The period between 12-36 months is critical for the baby's growth and development. There is a lot of change your baby needs to get accustomed to during this period. From learning new skills such as interacting with others or talking and walking, to becoming independent, this stage is all about growth.

Major Toddler Milestones

All the things that your little one can do will excite and surprise you. From the first step he takes to the words he utters and the real interactions through verbal and non-verbal communication, there is a lot to look forward to. There are critical milestones for every toddler, which determine his overall growth and progress. Usually, a baby takes his first steps around his first birthday, but this can also vary. No two individuals are alike, and the same stands true for toddlers too. The first milestone, you need to watch out for is when your baby learns to walk. This usually happens when the baby is between 12-18 months old. Parents often worry when their baby doesn't do things that other babies do. Don't be in a rush, and don't worry because they also grow at their own pace. As your baby grows, he will walk alone, run, and indulge in simple physical activities with objects such as playing with a ball or pulling his toys.

Between the ages of 10-14 months, babies utter their first words. Be a little patient, and you might need to listen to a lot of gibberish before he speaks real words. Even if your toddler isn't communicating using actual words, don't worry. Instead, look for other ways he's trying to communicate with you. Other forms of non-verbal communication include pointing, nodding his head, or even staring in a specific direction. It is also an age during which toddlers learn social and emotional skills that help them understand simple concepts such as making others laugh and associating names to their feelings and emotions.

Usually, here is the basic development; you might see your toddler when he is between 12-17 months old.

- Get attached to a stuffed toy or a blanket.
- Starts showing a preference for a specific hand (uses his dominant hand)

- Loves to play games
- Holds out his arms when you dress him
- Has probably perfected one or two simple words
- Understands the concept of a reflection he sees of himself in the mirror
- Can bend and pick up objects
- Can follow simple instructions
- Starts eating with fingers
- Points at objects
- Tries to stand up from a sitting position
- Grabs hold onto small objects.
- Starts scribbling
- Can chew bigger pieces of food
- Understands and obeys instructions
- Starts to run
- Shows preferences specific foods
- Tries to climb
- Shows an affinity for specific colors

Here are the basic developmental milestones you might see your toddler when he is between 18-36 months old.

- Might understand instructions but does not necessarily follow them
- Excitedly dances to music.
- Starts insisting on eating by himself
- Likes helping adults with their chores
- Can identify body parts such as eyes, nose, and mouth
- Stops putting different objects he picks up in his mouth
- Starts reading on his own, even if it sounds like gibberish
- Bedtime struggles start
- Understands the difference between right and wrong
- Can link two words together
- Starts undressing on his own
- Learns to throw a ball or other objects

- Starts to walk up and down the stairs slowly
- Has better communication skills
- Can brush teeth by himself
- Can identify objects or people in pictures
- Learns to understand the meaning of propositions
- Can show shyness
- Loves interactive games and stacking
- Wants a lot of attention
- Can identify his likes and dislikes
- Starts responding to basic questions and talks about himself

Common Toddler Troubles

Aggression

You might be worried when your toddler becomes aggressive and at his external displays of aggression through hitting or biting. As unpleasant as it sounds, it is common. It's often due to his desire to be independent. This, coupled with the fact that he cannot control his impulses and is just learning language skills, trigger his aggressive behavior. However, it doesn't mean all this is acceptable. You will learn more about dealing with undesirable behavior using positive parenting in the subsequent chapters.

Screaming

Some toddlers scream because they want attention, or they are denied something. Sometimes, toddlers shout to test their parents' boundaries. Screaming is your toddler's way of getting your attention, and it is something he desires.

Lying

Active imagination and forgetfulness are the two common reasons toddlers lie. Their inability to differentiate between reality and imagination can make it difficult for them to distinguish between what has or hasn't happened.

Tattling

It is believed toddlers often resort to tattling to get attention, increase their self-esteem, or display their power. It helps your child believes he has one-up another kid. He also wrongly believes that it makes him look more positive in the eyes of adults around him. They tattle because they haven't developed the emotional or social skills required to understand how to solve their problems.

Interrupting

Toddlers somehow believe the world revolves around them. Their short-term memory is still developing, and they strongly need to say things right away before they forget. This is one reason why they constantly interrupt others while talking. Also, the idea of interruptions does not exist in your toddler's head. Don't understand that others might want to say things or do things that are beyond their interest.

Throwing Tantrums

Another common problem during toddler years is tantrums. The toddler understands more verbal communication but is still not at a stage where he can freely communicate what he wants. This inability to communicate can make him feel helpless and results in tantrums.

Teasing

When your toddler is about two years old, he understands what boundaries mean, and he keeps testing them to understand where his limits are. Toddlers like teasing, but it's never with any malicious intentions. It is a sign of his cognitive development.

Whining

Your toddler depends on you for every basic need or desire, whether or not it is food or love - he relies on you. If he doesn't get your attention when he needs it, it becomes a challenge for him. This results in whining. The high pitch used during whining is his way of trying to get your attention when one of his needs hasn't been met.

Throwing Things

When a child is between 18-36 months old, he develops and fine-tunes his motor skills. A simple way he learns to do this is by picking up and throwing objects. Your toddler doesn't do this to irritate or annoy you. Instead, he thinks of it as an enjoyable activity and often does it to practice his motor skills.

None of these behaviors are desirable but are to be expected. You will learn more about fixing such behaviors and replacing them with desirable ones in the next chapters.

Chapter Two: What Is Positive Discipline?

Before learning about positive discipline, it's essential to understand the difference between discipline and punishment. These two terms are often used synonymously, but they couldn't be more different. Simply put, discipline involves positive methods that teach a child to be confident, responsible, and exert self-control. Instead of telling your child what he's not supposed to, it helps to teach him what is okay and what isn't okay. With discipline, you can teach your child new skills to regulate his behavior, problem-solving techniques, and deal with any unpleasantness. It enables him to learn from his mistakes and replace them with socially appropriate ways to handle himself. Instead of taking away his privileges, shouting or spanking, disciplining helps him avoid undesirable behaviors.

But punishment includes punitive measures. It essentially means you are giving your child a penalty for any misbehavior or offense. It's about making your child pay for his misbehaviors. At times, parents also punish their kids because they are frustrated. It can also stem from the desperation that the parent yells, spanks, or takes away a privilege given to his child. To send a message that his behavior needs to change or else he will be yelled, spanked, or his privileges will be taken away. The main problem with punishment is it doesn't teach good behavior. It might tell him he's not supposed to do something because he will be punished otherwise. He might feel confused about why it is okay for you as a parent to yell at him, but he is not supposed to do this.

Another major problem with punishment is it makes children feel out of control. When you teach appropriate behaviors and why certain behaviors are undesirable, it gives a better sense of control. It makes him feel like he in complete control of his actions and any natural consequences that follow either direct result of his actions.

Meaning of Positive Discipline

Dr. Jane Nelsen is accredited with creating the program of positive discipline. Her work relies heavily on the teachings of Alfred Adler and Rudolf Dreikurs. The idea behind positive discipline is to equip young people with the skills they need to become respectful, responsible, and resourceful members of the society. It helps teach quintessential life and social skills, which is respectful and encouraging for adults and children alike.

It is a natural human tendency to connect with others, and this desire is rather strong in children. Once your child feels this sense of connection to his family and others around him, chances are his misbehavior will reduce. Positive discipline is based on mutual respect, effective communication, problem-solving techniques, understanding the reasons for a specific behavior, encouragement, and concentrating on the solutions instead of the problem. Positive discipline teaches parents to be proactive instead of reactive. It's always easy to fix the situation before it worsens, instead of reacting to it when it's bad.

When you teach your child good behaviors and why certain behaviors are undesirable, exhibiting such behavior reduces. If you talk to him while he is calm and composed, he will be more likely to listen to you. If you try explaining all this to him when he's throwing a tantrum, it will merely worsen the situation.

Benefits of Positive Discipline

Positive discipline helps improve the bond between parents and children. It also strengthens the connection you share. If you continually punish your child, give him timeouts, take away his privileges, or shout at him, it strains the relationship. It can also create resentment in the kid. The tactics used for practicing positive discipline are mutually encouraging and respectful. You learn to be kind and firm to your child. Instead of punishing him, when you calmly explain why he's not supposed to do something, he probably will listen to you.

It is also effective in the long run. When your child knows what he's supposed to do and not supposed to, and the reasons for the same, it becomes easier to teach him good behaviors. When you punish him for any misbehavior, it merely illustrates that he isn't supposed to do something. However, it doesn't give him any skills or lessons essential for learning good behavior. Even if punishment works, the benefits it offers are only momentary.

Another advantage of positive discipline is it teaches children vital social and life skills such as respecting others, being considerate, learning to solve problems, and cooperating with others. All these skills will turn your child into an adult; you will respect, love unconditionally, and admire.

According to, "Relations Among Positive Parenting, Children Suffered Full Control, And Externalizing Problems: A Three-Wave Longitudinal Study," (2005) and "Intergenerational Continuity In Parenting Behavior: Mediating Partisan Child Effects" (2009) positive discipline helps foster emotional growth, but academic performance, improves mental health and provides better outcomes in terms of trials behavior.

Positive discipline also gives your child the chance to understand how capable he is. It helps build his self-esteem and confidence.

Principles of Positive Discipline

Positive discipline is a simple concept based on practicality. There are no standardized principles of positive discipline, but some ground rules need to be followed. In this section, let's look at the core principles of positive discipline.

Principle #1: Shift Focus

It is easy to say, "Don't do this," but it serves no purpose. Instead of harping on the things your toddler isn't supposed to do, positive discipline helps tell him what he can do. Instead of saying, "Don't run around the house," with positive discipline, you are taught to say, "Walk carefully instead of running." It also helps make the child understand why certain actions aren't desirable. If you catch your little one running carelessly, you can tell him, "If you run in the house, you can fall and hurt yourself." By explaining, it becomes easier to make him understand why certain behaviors aren't desirable.

Principle #2: The Child's Feelings

If your child makes a mistake or misbehaves, instead of getting upset with him and shouting or yelling, positive discipline teaches you to become more considerate about your child's feelings. No child is inherently bad. It is just the behavior that needs to be changed. If your child spills his food, don't say, "You are a bad boy!" Instead, you can concentrate on the action or behavior, which isn't desirable. If you criticize your child and constantly put him down or punish him, he will soon believe he isn't lovable or capable. As a parent, it is your job to ensure that your child's self-esteem and confidence don't take a back seat.

Principle #3: Offer A Choice

Everyone likes to be in control of their lives, decide and choose what they want. Well, toddlers are no different. They might not be fully-grown yet, but they understand what choice means and like choosing. A common mistake a lot of parents make is they give their children choices when interested in abiding by their decisions. With positive discipline, you're taught to offer your child the choice only when you are 100% willing to abide by his decision. The simplest way to do this is by giving the child choices acceptable to you. For instance, if your toddler throws a tantrum because he isn't allowed to play for longer, you can tell them something like, "If you have your dinner right now, you can play for 10 minutes later." You have given him a choice, which is acceptable to you. It also gives your toddler a sense of control.

Principle #4: Environment Matters

A child's behavior is often regulated by his environment. Instead of worrying too much about his behavior, concentrate on changing his environment. For instance, if your toddler's senses are constantly overstimulated because of a noisy environment, he will become cranky and throw tantrums. Understanding the cause of the tantrum- the environment- gives you more control of regulating his action. Now that you know he's throwing tantrums because he's overstimulated, you can reduce the stimulation from the environment.

Principle #5: You Are A Team

A simple principle lot of parents forget they need to work as a team with their children. If you work against a child, he will resist, and make the entire process seem like a struggle. Instead, once you work with your toddler as a team, it becomes easier to change his actions. Don't be a dictator but be a mentor. You and your child are a team and work together to change his behavior. For instance, if you are upset about your child's bedtime routine, instead of dictating terms, try to talk to him about it. With a little adjustment and understanding, you both can create a routine that works well for you. With positive discipline, you are taught how to do all this.

Principle #6: Setting Limits

We're taught that every function has a limit. What happens when a function has no limit? It either ceases to exist or doesn't work like it is supposed to. Likewise, even your toddler needs certain limits. Most limits set by parents are to regulate their toddler's behaviors are often designed, keeping their safety in mind. Ensure the limits you set up are something your child can understand. Once you set these limits, explain the consequences of breaking such limits, too. Let's assume one of the ground rules or the limits you set in the house for your toddler's safety is, "Don't run." To enforce this limit, explain what will happen if he doesn't listen to you. By explaining the importance of the limit, and the consequences of breaking it, it's more likely that your toddler will be more agreeable to following them.

It's not just about setting boundaries, but you need to be consistent too. If you are inconsistent, the child will get confused and not understand what he's supposed to do. For instance, if you tell him he isn't supposed to watch TV while eating, stick to this ground rule. No one is supposed to change this rule, regardless of the situation. There might be days when you are tired or exhausted and don't have the energy to get through dinnertime. However, it doesn't give you an excuse to allow your child to eat while watching TV. After a while, if you do this, he will soon believe there are no rules and no consequences of breaking any rules you set. With a little consistency, the child gets used to the limits. It's not just you who needs to follow these rules, although caregivers in your child's life should also be on board.

Principle #7: Gentle Reminders

Instead of demanding or ordering your toddler's compliance, you can use gentle reminders, questions, or even state facts to obtain his compliance. For instance, you might want your toddler to put his toys away after playtime. This might be a constant power struggle. There is a simple way to circumvent this. Instead of demanding his compliance by saying things such as, "You should put your toys away," or punishing him, "if you don't put your toys away, you cannot play," look for gentle reminders. Children resist because they don't like being told what to do. When you give them a command, their natural urge to resist increases. If you replace the command with a simple question or one-word reminder, it works better. To get your child to put his toys away after playtime, try reminding him, "Toys." Yes, all it takes is a single word. Instead of wasting your breath with long sentences and power struggles that leave you winded, try gentle reminders.

Principle #8: Be A Good Role Model

You are your child's first role model. Most of the behaviors that children pick up are often the culmination of all behaviors they notice in their environment. As the primary caregiver in your child's life, it's important to portray good behavior. For instance, if your child screams or shouts whenever he doesn't get something he wants, as a parent, fix this behavior. If you shout whenever you don't get something you want, you are merely contradicting what you told your child. It also causes a lot of unnecessary confusion for the kids. If you don't want your child to scream and shout, you need to model the same behavior. If he sees you doing something you told him not to, he will soon believe he need not listen to you.

Once you follow these principles and incorporate them into your parenting tactics, it becomes easier to guide your child and mold his behavior. Instead of punishing him whenever he misbehaves, positive discipline helps teach him why such behavior is undesirable. It helps shift the focus from punishments to changing his behavior for the better.

A Simple Exercise in Positive Discipline

What is misbehavior? It is the term used to describe rude, bad, or improper behavior. Only when your child consciously behaves inappropriately will such behavior be termed as misbehavior.

Before you act upon it or fix it, here are simple questions you should ask yourself.

Question 1: Did my child misbehave? Did he do something wrong?

Do you think there is a problem, or maybe you are running low on energy and patience? Often, parents get upset with their children's behavior, especially when stressed, overwhelmed, or are running low on energy. For instance, there might have been instances in your past when you were upset with your toddler because he didn't put his toys away after playtime like he is supposed to. Your reaction in the situation would be different if you are overwhelmed and stressed compared to your regular reactions. If you think there is no problem, it's time to look within yourself and understand the reason for the stress and deal with it. If you strongly believe there is a problem, it brings us to the next question.

Question 2: Can my child live up to my expectations?

If there seems to be a problem, think about it for a couple of minutes. We all have certain expectations. Most problems we face in life are due to such expectations. Likewise, all parents have certain expectations. Before you get upset with your child's behavior, ask yourself:

Am I realistic about my expectations? Can my child live up to my expectations? If your expectations aren't realistic, it is time for a little reevaluation. If you believe your expectations are fair and reasonable, move on to the next question.

Question 3: Was your child aware that he was doing something wrong?

Go back and reconsider the definition of misbehavior. Actions cannot be termed as misbehavior if they are not done consciously. Therefore, try to determine if your child knew whether he was misbehaving or not. If he was unaware that he did something wrong, there is no reason to get upset with him. Instead, try to understand the following.

- What happened
- What wasn't supposed to happen
- What you expect of him and the reasons
- How it can be avoided in the future
- To prevent such behaviors in the future, offer your help and assistance

If he knew he was doing something that he wasn't supposed to and still went ahead with intentionally, it means your child misbehaved. If your child accidentally wets his bed while sleeping, it isn't an intentional act or misbehavior. If it was an accident, ask him why he did it.

Children are smarter than parents give them credit for. If you get down to his level and talk to him, he will tell you what's happening in his way. Learn to be patient with your little one, guide him, and don't punish.

Chapter Three: Positive Parenting Starts At Home (And With YOU)

Visualize this scenario: A 3-year-old toddler is throwing a tantrum because mommy cut her sandwiches as triangles instead of rectangles. She thrashes and throws up her hands and screams and cries. It seems like this tantrum will not end soon. Out of sheer frustration, the mom shouts, "Stop screaming right NOW."

Does the scenario seem familiar to you? No matter how much you love your little one and the patience you have, sometimes, calming down your toddler seems impossible. Well, all parents have been there. It's something we are all guilty of doing so don't be too hard on yourself. In the previous chapters, you introduced to the concept of positive discipline, and in this chapter, you will learn about simple ways to get started with that.

Tips to Get Started with Positive Parenting

Understand the Reasons

Why do toddlers misbehave? This is an important question all parents must ask themselves. There's always a reason for their misbehavior, even if it seems silly to you. Adults might believe the reasons to be silly, but it probably feels reasonable to the child, and that's why they behave the way they do. The simplest way to ensure any misbehavior is fixed is by finding the reason. By addressing the cause directly, you can better understand your child's needs while making him feel acknowledged and understood. Even if it doesn't solve the problem immediately, it gives your child a reason to move on without resorting to any misbehavior. Once you understand the reason, it also gives you better control over the scenario and takes the required steps to prevent the repetition of such behavior.

For instance, a toddler cries when his sibling hits him. The older sibling hit him because the little one took away his toys without asking. This is a teaching moment for both the kids. You can teach the younger one to always ask for permission before taking others' things. Similarly, you can teach the older child to regulate his emotions and talk about his feelings without physically lashing out. By teaching them the right behavior, you can reduce the chances of such instances.

Learn to be Kind and Firm

Kids often learn by mimicking the behavior of those around them, especially their primary caregivers. If a parent shouts, yells, calls the child names, or spanks him, the child soon learns it's okay to do these things when he is upset. The opposite of this is true too. As a parent, once you start showcasing kind and respectful behavior towards others, even when you are upset, it teaches your toddler to deal with a difficult situation, while being kind and respectful. When you are calm, even in difficult circumstances, it helps calm the child and increases his ability to understand what you are telling him.

Remember, there is a difference between being kind and giving in to your child's demands. A common misunderstanding is parents believe that positive discipline is like permissive parenting. Permissive parenting means giving into a child's demands whether they are reasonable or not. Don't be mean to get your point across. Learning to be kind and firm is a great way to communicate with your toddler while teaching him good behaviors. Saying no firmly and calmly is better than shouting the same at your child. Whenever you set any limits about specific behaviors such as no hitting, biting, or shouting, ensure you enforce the consequences if the rule is broken. It teaches the child about the natural relationship between actions or behaviors and their consequences. It enables the toddler to understand how to make decisions in the future.

For instance, a family rule you can establish is "No shouting or screaming." The next time your toddler shouts or screams because he didn't get something or he wants something, ignore him until he calms down. It effectively teaches him that unless he asks for something calmly and respectfully, he will not get it.

Parents Need a Timeout Too!

It isn't just the kids who need a timeout, but even parents need timeouts. Sometimes, you are tired, frustrated, irritated, or even annoyed by your child's behavior. In such instances, instead of reacting, it's better to take a timeout. Even if it's a break for about five minutes, it helps calm you down. Once you are calm, it becomes easier to deal with your child's unruly behavior. If you lose your temper in that moment and shout at him, it sends conflicting messages about not shouting when upset. Remember, the behavior you portray needs to be in harmony with the rules you set, and the established consequences.

Once you are calm, you can talk to your child about the problem. This is a good example of a teachable moment of "Do as I say, and as I do." Do you want your child to scream and shout when he's angry or upset, or do you want him to control his emotions and stay respectful? If it's the latter, you need to do the same. If you think you are about to lose it, calmly tell your child you need a couple of moments to compose yourself. Give him a timeframe of when you will come back and talk to him about the issue. The simplest way to avoid unnecessary power struggles is by walking away from the issue. Take a few deep breaths, calm yourself, and clear your mind.

Don't Be Punitive

One of the basic concepts of positive discipline and positive parenting is not to punish the child. Whenever you punish the child, it builds up a feeling of resentment, rebellion, revenge, and increases the risk of him retreating. Punishment condemns bad behavior, but it doesn't teach good or desirable behavior. Instead of doing all this, it's always better to look for nonpunitive options. A positive timeout or a time-in is a great way to implement the principles of positive discipline. A positive timeout is the exact opposite of a conventional timeout. This is not a form of punishment. In the previous chapter, it was mentioned that a child's poor behavior could be due to a stimulating environment. By using the principle of time in, you are essentially removing the child from the problematic environment. It gives your toddler a chance to calm down and stop the undesirable behavior finally.

To use a timeout, the first step is always to explain your expectations and the consequences of not meeting such expectations. For instance, if your toddler hits the family pet, tell him that such behavior will result in a timeout. Once you establish this rule and its likely consequence, it gives your toddler a chance to think about his behavior and decisions before making them. It also teaches him how to make good choices and develop his cognitive thinking abilities. If your child exhibits undesirable behavior, don't lose your cool, and calmly tell him what he did was on the right and let him sit in a quiet and safe place. Give him the time to think about his actions and the resultant consequence. Instead of being punitive, you are essentially kind and firm while correcting any undesirable behavior.

Another important thing about a time-in is you need to talk to your toddler after it ends. Explain why his previous action was undesirable or inappropriate and help him develop a better response if he experiences the same feelings in the future. This is easier said than done and requires a lot of practice and patience.

Clarity and Consistency

As your child's primary caregiver, it is your responsibility to be clear, consistent, and follow through on your promises. Before you enforce a rule, ensure that you have explained the rule to your little one and have also explained the consequences of not following the rules. Remember, the rules need to be quite small, and the consequences simple. Your toddler is still learning, and his brain is developing. If you are inconsistent, it merely creates a lot of confusion. For instance, parents often make empty threats to regulate their child's misbehavior. If you say, "No more toys for a week," when your toddler runs in the house, ensure it isn't an empty threat. If, after a day, you let him play with the toys, your threat has no value. (P.s. This isn't a good idea because it's a punishment and will not teach him good behavior and is merely an example of empty threats parents make).

If you don't follow through on what you say, your child will soon realize he need not listen to you. To avoid all this, you need to talk the talk and walk the walk too.

Learn, Learn, and Learn

Whenever your child misbehaves, don't get frustrated or worried. Instead, think of it as a teaching moment. Let us assume your toddler throws his brand-new toy during a temper tantrum. Instead of punishing him for this behavior, calmly take the toy away and don't replace it. This teaches him that breaking a toy doesn't make a new toy magically appear. Don't allow him to play with it, and certainly do not replace it. It teaches him the natural consequence of his action. The simplest way for a toddler to understand the difference between good and bad behavior is through experiences. This simple exercise will teach him that throwing his toys doesn't solve the problem, and it merely means he no longer gets to play with it.

This is also a good opportunity for you to teach him feeling words. He might not understand the words and their meanings yet, but through repetition, it becomes easier to teach different emotions he might be experiencing.

Always be Patient

Don't expect any drastic behavioral changes overnight. If this is one of your expectations, you are merely setting yourself up for disappointment. Learn to manage your expectations and consider your child's age. Remember, he is still a toddler and is learning. His prefrontal cortex, a part of the brain responsible for making sound judgments and understanding the true implication of consequences, is still in the developing stage. Therefore, it's quintessential you are patient with him. Repetition, consistency, and effort are important to teach your child good behavior and discourage undesirable behaviors. The great thing about implementing the principles of positive parenting is that it offers lifelong rewards.

As your child's primary caregiver, positive discipline also teaches you to learn to regulate your emotions and behaviors to more effectively communicate with your toddler.

Positive Discipline Techniques

Besides using time-ins, timeouts for parents, consistency, and patience, you can try some simple positive discipline techniques.

Provide Options

One effective way to encourage independence in a child from a young age is to provide options. Engaging in power struggles is seldom an efficient way to encourage good behavior; instead, it merely creates a lot of personal tiffs and unpleasantness. If you offer your child choices instead of barking commands or orders, you can avoid power struggles. This technique also helps empower your toddler. Are you wondering how this technique is an effective way of parenting? Well, you need to be smart about the choices you offer. Never offer your child choices you wouldn't follow. If you do this, it merely makes you seem inconsistent and unreliable. Instead, the choices should be simple and age-appropriate.

For instance, if you are getting ready to go out, instead of shouting at your child and saying, "We are getting late again, move it" you can say something like, "Do you want to put on your jacket first, or put on your shoes first??" In this situation, you are not concentrating on the action; instead, you are trying to move things along by giving your child choices. Both these choices are perfectly acceptable to you because it helps reduce the time he spends getting dressed. Since children love autonomy, this technique works brilliantly well.

Creating A YES Environment

Humans are naturally curious, and this curiosity is high in children. This curiosity helps them explore their surroundings and learn more about themselves and those around them. As a baby grows, his instinct of self-expression increases. This is the reason toddlers often test boundaries and push their parent's limits. It's their way of asserting their sense of freedom and understanding their environment. If a parent keeps saying, "No," all the time, the child will soon feel discouraged. Your toddler might think he is not supposed to do anything, because everything is forbidden. Instead, look for creative ways to create a healthy and safe "Yes" environment. For instance, if you have a toddler at home, baby-proofing the house is a great way to ensure the household environment is safe for your toddler to explore different things.

Your toddler's willingness to pay attention to the things you are saying increases if you don't keep discouraging him from things. For instance, if your toddler constantly breaks glass articles at home, the best thing to do is lock them up. This reduces the chances of any misbehavior, and you don't even have to say no.

Ignore Negative Behavior

Toddlers love attention; not just toddlers - all humans love attention! From a toddler's perspective, attention is good, regardless of the actions that create it. Children act out because they get the attention they think they deserve from their parents or caregivers. In such situations, the best thing you can do is ignore their negative behavior. If your child is throwing a tantrum, for no apparent reason, and all his needs are taken care of, ignore his negative behavior. He will soon tire of it and realize he will not get the attention he wants through displaying negative behavior. This technique should be used only for minor problems and nothing significant.

Fictional Characters Help

There are a lot of teaching moments while parenting a toddler. A great way to engage your toddler and teach him positive behavior (while discouraging negative behavior) is by using fictional characters. Third-party mediators, such as a puppet, toy, or characters from his favorite TV show, can be used effectively. Put up a small puppet show for your child showing good behaviors that should be used instead of undesirable ones. For instance, one puppet could hit the other while the other cries. In this situation, you can carefully explain that instead of hitting the puppet, had he merely asked the other what he wants, the situation could have been better handled. By using means of communication your toddler understands, it becomes easier to teach him good manners.

Single-Word Reminders

Most parents wrongly assume that stating their demands is the best way to get their toddlers to listen. Shouting or sternly saying, "Put your toys away!" "Stop running right now!" doesn't get the message across. Besides leaving you hoarse, it might serve no purpose at all. Instead, try using single word reminders. A principle of positive discipline is not just to fix any undesirable behavior but also to teach desirable ones. Try saying, "Walk," whenever you notice your toddler is running or if he has a tough time sharing his toys, you can say "Share." These simple reminders stated calmly will effectively convey your message while telling your toddler what he's supposed to do.

Always remember to choose your battles wisely in life; parenting is no exception. Instead of engaging in unnecessary power struggles, it is better to gently correct and redirect your child to learn better behavior.

Positive Reinforcement

Correct undesirable behavior, but also praise your toddler whenever he does something desirable. If your toddler picks up his toys after playtime with no reminders, praise his behavior using simple sentences like, "You did a good job!" or "Thank you for picking up your toys." If he is kind to others or shares his toys with his sibling, tell him, "You did great," or "I am so happy you shared your toys." Whenever you notice your toddler doing something you appreciate, convey this appreciation to him.

Stating positive statements while expressing positive emotions acts as an incentive. He will soon realize that certain behaviors will elicit a happy response from you. By giving him positive attention for his good behavior, you are reinforcing the behavior he displayed. Positive reinforcement also helps build your child's self-esteem and self-confidence. He will soon realize he can make good decisions with no external assistance. It might not seem like much to you, but it does help change and mold his behavior for the better. If a parent keeps shouting or snapping at their child for misbehaving, but doesn't reward good behavior, the child will feel discouraged sooner or later. Chances are he will withdraw himself into a shell, resent his parent, or even rebel unnecessarily.

Redirection

The attention span of a toddler is short. Whenever your toddler misbehaves, quickly redirect him to another activity. When you redirect him, it diverts his attention and effectively ends any bad behavior. For instance, if you notice your toddler is playing with something he's not supposed to, give him another toy to redirect his attention. If this technique doesn't work, you can shift from one room to another. Keep practicing the same tactic as your child grows. For instance, if you don't want your toddler watching television all the time, you can tell him he can play with his toys or take him outdoors for a while. Instead of telling him he's not supposed to do something, direct him towards a positive activity.

By following these simple techniques of positive discipline, you can effectively prevent misbehavior, encourage desirable behavior, and help your child cultivate good habits while increasing his self-confidence.

Chapter Four: Sleep Training for Your Toddler

Sleep training isn't an aspect a lot of parents even think about when they welcome their little one into their lives. However, once the baby is home, the constant feedings, diaper changes, and all the other usual responsibilities of life can quickly become overwhelming. This is when the reality of this new life sets in. Instead of the "I'll just wing it" approach, it is better to have a plan in mind. The simplest way to rectify this situation is by sleep- training your toddler. Once your toddler is sleep-trained, even you can get sufficient rest to keep doing your best as a parent.

In this chapter, you will learn about the two simple methods of sleep training, tips for using positive parenting during sleep training, and dealing with common bedtime struggles.

How to Sleep Train Your Toddler

Essentially, sleep training is teaching your toddler to sleep through the night. Initially, he might resist and will probably wake up after a couple of hours. However, if you keep at it, your toddler will soon learn to sleep through the night without disturbances.

Experts suggest it's usually ideal to start sleep training your baby when he is around 4-6 months old. By this age, babies usually have a sleep-wake routine, and the nighttime feedings also stop altogether or reduce drastically. Since no two babies are alike, don't be worried if your little one takes a while longer for sleep training. If you are unsure if your baby is ready for this step, consult a pediatrician.

So, what is the best option available for sleep training a toddler? The answer to this question depends on how your baby responds to each option; you should also be comfortable with the chosen strategy. Different experts have different opinions, and the best method is a widely debated topic. However, one thing everyone seems to agree on is the need for consistency. To sleep-train your baby, pick a strategy, and stick with it while leaving little room for flexibility. Based on your baby's responses to it, you can make the required changes. Let's learn about some different methods available.

Longer And Longer Method

If you leave the toddler in the crib or put him down for sleep on his bed and walk away, he probably cries. He is crying because he isn't used to being alone. Those who advocate this method suggest it's okay for a baby to cry until he learns to sleep. Never let your toddler cry for indefinite periods. In this method, you essentially put your toddler to bed while he is wide awake. However, even when he cries, you shouldn't comfort him or pick him up. Instead, you merely let him cry out and tire himself to sleep. This method was popularized by Richard Ferber, a pediatrician associated with the Centre for Pediatric Sleep Disorders. According to Ferber's method, it's believed the baby or toddler will sooner or later learn to soothe himself to sleep with no external support. Even if he cries for a while, he will soon put himself to sleep once he realizes no one is coming to comfort him.

This method might sound a little harsh, but it's been used for ages – and is effective. Once again, whether you want to use this method will depend on your comfort level. If your toddler cries incessantly without stopping, don't forget to check on him. Advocates suggest it will not be a traumatic experience for the baby if you let him cry himself to sleep while regularly checking on him.

No-Tears Approach

If you are uncomfortable with the previous method or it didn't work for your baby (showing no positive change within two weeks), it's time to try something new. Unlike the previous method, this approach is gradual, slowly getting your toddler accustomed to sleeping through the night without difficulty. This method is foundational upon a well-structured bedtime routine, allowing you to connect with your baby by using a comforting bedtime ritual, quickly tending to any of his requests for comfort. It will make your baby feel loved and secure while he sleeps on his own.

Start by teaching a simple-yet-consistent nap routine your toddler can follow during the day. If you regulate his naps during the day, it becomes easier to regulate his sleeping schedule at night. Try to put your toddler to sleep a little earlier than usual. Aim for anywhere between 6:30 and 7:30 PM. Many parents commonly err by allowing their toddlers to stay awake for longer, believing they will tire themselves out. Avoid this misconception! If you allow your toddler to stay past his ideal bedtime, it will merely make him cranky and increase unpleasant interactions. When you allow your baby to stay awake for longer, he'll become accustomed to staying awake at night and sleeping through the day. Simply put, if your baby is overtired or overstimulated, he cannot fall asleep at night.

Since this method is about making gradual changes, first establish an ideal bedtime for him. For instance, if your baby usually sleeps at 8:30-9 PM, don't drastically reduce it to 6:30 or 7:30 PM Instead, reduce it by 30 minutes. Keep doing this until you reach your desired time for his bedtime.

The next step is to create a relaxing and comforting bedtime ritual. Once the ritual is in place, ensure that you follow it consistently. For instance, include a warm bath, story time, lullaby, or even light music. After this, you can dim the lights, change his clothes, and put him down to sleep. The routine needs to be consistent, and there should be no deviations. This routine is not only for you; every primary caregiver in your toddler's life should follow this routine – no matter of where he is.

Come up with a phrase, word, or even a sound that acts as an external cue to signal your baby's bedtime. For instance, you can say "Shhh" gently or even use a phrase such as "It is bedtime," or "It is nighty-night-time" while you are trying to put your baby to sleep. Keep repeating this phase, word, or sound. After a while, an association will be formed in your toddler's mind, reminding him that he needs to sleep whenever you use your cue.

Another important aspect: the sleeping environment. Ensure your toddler is comfortable whenever you put him to bed. If the environment is too loud, bright, or noisy, it will overstimulate your toddler's senses, preventing him from effectively falling asleep. You can also use a white noise machine as a part of his bedtime ritual. It helps mask any background noises while creating a soothing environment, which is often helpful. While he is about to fall asleep, play some soothing music, sing a lullaby, or even read a small bedtime story. Making a bedtime story a part of his sleeping ritual gives you a chance to bond with him. Make the most of these moments because the bond you establish with him during childhood (especially early childhood), is unlike anything else.

While using this method, pay attention to his sleepy whimpers and real cries. It can be tempting to check on your little one whenever you hear any sounds from his room. Unless it's a genuine cry, don't do this. If you keep disturbing him while he's trying to sleep, he won't learn to fall asleep. However, you can check on him after an hour or two during the initial phases. Use this method to increase the time between the nighttime check-ins gradually.

Positive Parenting and Sleep Training

Here is a scenario a lot of parents might be familiar with. It is about 8 PM, and it is two-year-old Adam's bedtime. The mother says, "Adam, it is time to go to bed immediately." However, Adam seems to have other plans. He shrieks "No," and heads for the playroom. The mother follows him and says, "Adam, honey, it is time for you to sleep. Please come." Adam is vehemently shaking his head "no" and continues to play with his toys. This is the last straw, and the mother loses her cool. She picks up Adam, and he wiggles, squeals and shrieks while flailing his arms. She says, "Stop it immediately, or else!" This sends Adam into overdrive as he redoubles his efforts to get away from his mom. He cries even louder, and the emotional and physical struggle for power continues. The mother somehow gets him to brush his teeth, change his pajamas, kiss him, and puts him to bed.

Phew, she breathes a sigh of relief, thinking tonight's battle is over. Before she takes ten steps, she hears her toddler say, "Mommy, I need water." Resigned, the mother gives him the drink of water. By now, she is frustrated and tired. After this, she stiffly says, "Go to sleep now. I don't want to hear another word from you. Good night!" This leaves the two-year-old Adam crying into his pillow while he struggles to sleep.

Does this scenario sound familiar? A lot of parents might find it hard to believe, but they aren't alone; these power struggles are common. Instead of making bedtime seem like a harsh punishment or an unpleasant routine, you can quickly fix this situation by using positive discipline. While using the previous sleep training methods, here are simple things you can remember to reduce any troubles you face in this process.

If you engage in such unpleasant power struggles, it will soon take a toll on the bond you share with your toddler. It will leave you feeling guilty and frustrated while the toddler feels misunderstood. So, the simple idea is to look at the situation from his perspective.

If you look at this situation from the toddler's perspective, it gives you a better understanding of why he behaved the way he did. He was playing with his toys and having a good time. Then, an adult comes in and tells him to stop and go to sleep. Even when he said no, the adult does not listen to him. Instead, he was merely picked up and made to go through the bedtime ritual. He wasn't ready yet and was forced into doing all this. Imagine if someone did all this to you. We all expect our wishes to be respected; the toddler is no different. Instead of engaging in power struggles, it's better to understand how he might be feeling. You would feel violated, angry, frustrated, and even controlled if the roles were reversed. Many parents fail to understand that even though their toddler is not an adult, he can feel all this, like any other human.

He is an individual, wanting to be respected and understood. If you take this power away from him, it becomes difficult for him to express himself. He puts up a fight because he isn't tired or sleepy, and he doesn't enjoy feeling controlled. We don't like being ordered around either! Remember this when dealing with your toddler. Instead of commanding your toddler to do something that merely escalates the situation, there is more you can do.

Make it Special

A bedtime ritual can be a special time for bonding and strengthening the closeness and connectedness between parents and toddlers. Usually, parents are tired during the day, and at night, they are eager to tuck their little ones to sleep. For a parent, completing this task gives them a break from daily rituals and offers quiet time. However, it conveys the wrong message to the toddler. The toddler might believe his parents are trying to get rid of him by putting him to sleep. In the previous scenario, Adam's desire for a glass of water before going to bed was his way of spending more time with his mother. So, why does a child put up a fight before sleeping? It's his declaration of independence, he wants to feel closer to his parent, wants to have a sense of control over whatever happens in his life, and wants to be heard and respected.

To ensure your child goes to sleep without struggles and all his needs and wants are satisfied, *respect your needs.* You are a human and not a tireless machine. Unless you take care of yourself during the day, you cannot deal with your child's bedtime ritual without feeling frazzled. Ensure that your child's bedtime leaves you at least an hour of downtime. Once you put your toddler to bed, you need time to relax and unwind. Ideally, always start the bedtime ritual about 45 minutes to an hour before his actual bedtime. For instance, if your toddler's bedtime is 8:30 PM, start this ritual at about 7:45 PM. Also, whenever possible, both the parents should try and participate in this process. It helps bond, while eliminating unnecessary power struggles.

Routine is quintessential for a baby between the ages of 12-24 months. This provides a sense of safety and security. It's always ideal to offer your child two choices instead of commanding him to do something. It gives him control over what happens to him. For instance, you can respect his sense of time by telling him he has another 10-20 minutes of playtime left before time for sleeping. Once it's time to start the bedtime ritual, you can ask him, "Do you want to sleep with a stuffed toy or a pillow?" "Do you want to change into your batman or dinosaur pajamas?" or "Do want me, or daddy, to help you with bath time?" "Do you want to listen to a lullaby or read a story together?" "How many kisses do you want before sleeping?" In all these instances, you are essentially offering a choice where either outcome is desirable for you.

After this, you can talk to him for a few minutes about his day; what he liked most and what he didn't enjoy. Take his advice into consideration as you structure his routine. Once you have gone through all these steps, it's time to end the bedtime ritual. Remember, you shouldn't talk to him after the ritual ends. Simply leave his room after saying a pleasant good night. If your child wakes up as soon as you leave the room and returns to you, gently guide him to his bed again. Don't be harsh or stern. Instead, lovingly tell him it's time for him to sleep. You can expect such behavior during the initial days of sleep training. However, after a while, he will get used to it.

How to Deal with Nightmares and Night Terrors

The terms "nightmare" and "night terrors" might sound the same, but they aren't. Learning to deal with your toddler's nightmares and night terrors is important to tackle the problem properly. Usually, kids as young as two years can have nightmares and night terrors. These two things are commonly used by the brain to process information and emotions. They go away as the child grows.

Any unpleasant or bad, yet realistic dreams are known as toddler nightmares and disturb your little one's sleep. Your toddler might remember and recollect his nightmare once awake. He might want to discuss it with you too. Naturally, he will have a tough time falling asleep after having a nightmare. Nightmares commonly occur during the lighter stage of REM (rapid eye movement) sleep, during the early hours of each day.

Night terrors are different in subtle ways. Don't be surprised if your child seems wide-awake with his eyes open and is screaming, sleepwalking, thrashing around, panting, or sweating heavily, *while asleep*. Your toddler might scream your name, but he might not sense or feel your presence fully. You might fully remember such incidents, but your child will not. Night terrors usually occur during the deep stages of non-REM sleep. They can last for up to 45 minutes, and your toddler may fall asleep right after it.

The first step towards learning how to deal with your toddler's nightmares and night terrors is to understand the difference between them. Your toddler might even seem a little restless during the dream state, but once he is awake, he will cry, panic, or scream. He will want to be comforted by you and express himself verbally and use his words to explain what he experienced.

If your toddler is having night terrors, even when he seems wide-awake, he's fast asleep. Even if you comfort him, he cannot sense your comforting presence during a night terror. Also, he would have no recollection of such episodes.

Different reasons could cause nightmares and night terrors in kids. A common factor is children have a tough time understanding to differentiate between reality and make-believe. Any stress or anxiety they experience during their waking hours can trigger nightmares or night terrors. For instance, maybe your toddler saw a scary looking bug, is overwhelmed due to the recent move to a new city, there is a change in your work schedule, or any other major life changes. Once you deal with the underlying fear and anxiety, nightmares and night terrors will both go away.

Any erratic changes in your toddler's sleeping patterns, illness, the lack of sleep – or even certain medications – can trigger them. It's commonly believed that frequent episodes of night terrors are often associated with a family history of the same. Remember, your toddler is processing a lot of information and trying to come to terms with the reality of life. Since there is a lot to process, his senses can be overstimulated, and all this information follows him into the dream world. The duration of a toddler's sleep cycle increases with age. This also opens a window for longer dreams and, perhaps, nightmares.

If your toddler seems to be having a nightmare, the best thing you can do is comfort him with gentle, soothing, and loving phrases; even making soothing sounds will make him feel safe and secure. You can help him settle back down for sleep after a nightmare by reassuring him that everything is all right. Saying, "It was just a dream, go back to sleep, honey," might not explain enough to a two-year-old who seems startled. Instead, you can help, "Honey, you were just playing pretend in your sleep." You could also make a show of checking dark spaces in his room, such as under the bed or in the closet.

Don't minimize your child's fears. It might not be scary to you, but it is surely scary to him! Also, you might be tempted to take him back to your room and sleep in the bed with you. Avoid doing this.

Instead, spend some more time calming him to sleep. There are simple ways to reduce the chance of a nightmare, such as ensuring your toddler has a soothing bedtime ritual, leaving a nightlight on, or leaving the bedroom door slightly ajar. Don't read any scary stories or allow your little one to watch scary movies right before bedtime.

Night terrors are not usually a permanent condition and go away within a few weeks. You cannot do much to stop night terrors or comfort your little one during the night terror. Attempting to wake up your little one from his night terror would leave him feeling disoriented, agitated, and confused. Likewise, don't try to hold him – even if he seems wide-awake. If he is awake, he will contact you. Instead, if he cries, shouts, and thrashes around, it's better to let the night terror run its course. Since he cannot recollect or even remember what happened, it's likely he will go back to sleep once the night terror has run its course. Don't mention anything about the night terror the following day.

The best thing you can do to deal with a night terror is to ensure there is no stress or underlying anxiety in your child's life. Spend more time with your little one, aim for quality time together as a family, and indulge in activities he enjoys, such as reading books together, cuddling, or even bathing. Try to get his sleep schedule back on track and avoid daytime naps.

Before you seek medical help, it would be ideal for maintaining a diary to track the frequency of his nightmares and night terrors. Keep track of the time when he goes to bed, the sleep he gets every night, if he requires any object for falling asleep, the number of times he wakes up, and the duration of each break from his sleep, the number of naps during the day, and any potential triggers for nightmares. If you have tried everything to deal with his stress and anxiety, it's time to seek medical help. A pediatrician could use the information in your sleep diary to detect the problem. There isn't much you can do to stop either a nightmare or a night terror, but you can be a comforting presence in your toddler's life.

How to Deal with Bedwetting

According to "Bedwetting In US Children: Epidemiology And Related Behavior Problems" (1996), about 30% of children under the age of five years by their beds in the US alone. Most children are potty trained between two to four years, but they might not be able to stay dry at day or night until they are older. Bedwetting isn't a problematic medical condition, but it can be challenging for parents and children. Before you learn to deal with bedwetting, it's important to understand what causes it. Here are some of the probable causes of bedwetting:

- The child might be an extremely sound sleeper and doesn't wake up, even when his bladder is full.
- He probably hasn't learned how to control his bladder movements, and the connection between his brain and bladder is developing.
- The child drinks a lot of water before going to sleep, and therefore, his body produces more urine at night.
- There might be a history of bedwetting in the family. Usually, it's believed that if a child is prone to bedwetting, it's probably because one or both his parents have the same problem as a child.
- The child is ill, tired, or isn't coping well with any stress or changes at home.
- The child's bladder is small and cannot hold all the urine produced overnight.
- The final cause may be an underlying medical condition.

While you are potty training your toddler, he might have a few accidents, which isn't uncommon. He might even go for days, weeks, and months before he has an accident. If this happens, it's nothing to worry about, and you merely need to stay patient. You'll learn more about potty training your toddler in the next chapter. For now, let's concentrate on bedwetting problems. If your child has an accident after weeks of potty training, start again.

Here are questions you should consider if you're concerned about your toddler's bedwetting or your toddler has complained about it.

- Is bedwetting a family problem?
- How frequently and when does your toddler pee during the day?
- Have there been any major changes or stress at home, such as shifting to a new city, welcoming a new baby, or even marital problems?
- Does your toddler consume a lot of fluids before bedtime?
- Is there anything unusual about your toddler's urine?
- If you have successfully potty trained your toddler for six months or more and starts bedwetting, it might be due to an underlying medical condition. Some medical troubles can trigger bedwetting suddenly are listed below:
  - Changes in the frequency and timing of when your toddler urinates during the day
  - If there's any disturbance with his gait, it could be a symptom of an underlying neurological condition.
  - There is continuous dampness.
  - The toddler is prone to bedwetting during the day and night.
  - Complains about a painful burning sensation while peeing.
  - Constant dribbling of a narrow stream of urine even after peeing.
  - Pink or cloudy urine coupled with faint bloodstains on his underpants.

If you notice any of these signs, you need to seek medical attention immediately. These signs are often associated with any kidney or bladder trouble.

How to Manage Bedwetting?

There are simple and practical tips you can use to deal with your toddler's bedwetting successfully.

Regardless of what happens, or how tired you are, do not blame him. If you shout, yell, or belittle, it will scare and scar him. He will soon believe bedwetting is a bad thing, and he will be punished. All these things will further worsen the problem.

Learn to be sensitive to his feelings. If you make a big issue of his bedwetting accidents, he will feel embarrassed. This merely increases the embarrassment he feels after the accident. Therefore, don't make a big deal out of it and deal with it as calmly and positively. Remind him it is okay and that it isn't a bad thing.

Talk to him and be honest while addressing the situation. When you explain it isn't his fault and how most children have accidents growing up, he will feel better.

If you create a positive environment, it becomes easier to deal with the issue. One simple way to do this is by teaching him responsibility. If he wets the bed, encourage him to help you while you clean. He need not change the sheets, but he could merely move the pillows or a stuffed toy. By giving him some responsibility, he will feel more in control of the situation.

Another way to deal with it is by protecting the bed with a plastic cover over the mattress. to protect it. Do this if you are aware that your child has had bedwetting instances.

It's not just about you creating a positive environment, but everyone in the household should abide by this rule. No one should make fun of the toddler, and there should be no teasing. He probably feels embarrassed about it, and if others tease or make fun of him, he will feel worse. Such behavior from adults can worsen their bedwetting problems.

To reduce any instances of bedwetting, avoid giving your toddler a big drink before going to bed. Also, ensure he empties his bladder before sleeping. While dealing with it, you can wake him up once or twice at night and encourage him to pee. Prevention is better than cure.

How to Stop Co-Sleeping

Many parents decide to co-sleep with their infants because it's the best way to get sufficient sleep during the first couple of months. However, this isn't ideal. Whether it's for your convenience, or to promote attachment, co-sleeping is not good, especially if you want your toddler to become independent and self-reliant. If your toddler is used to co-sleeping with you for years, getting used to sleeping on his own isn't easy. The sooner you start, the easier it becomes.

To stop co-sleeping with your newborn to 18-month-old, get him used to sleep in the crib or bassinet. Whenever he needs to sleep, put him down for a nap in this space, and *nowhere else*. It might be tempting to snuggle with your little one in bed, especially when he keeps waking up for feeding or peeing. Make it a point to not cuddle with your little one on the bed until you successfully stopped co-sleeping.

Slowly transition your baby, and ensure he has a safe place to sleep. The room shouldn't be too dark, place his blankets, pillows, and stuffed toys in his sleep space. You can also use a white noise machine to ensure there are no background noises, which will keep him up. Whether you are Ferberizing or using the no-tears approach, you must teach your baby to fall asleep independently. Use the tips discussed in the previous sections to create a soothing bedtime ritual while you transitioned from co-sleeping to sleeping in his crib or bassinet.

How can you stop co-sleeping with your baby between the ages of 18-48-months? If your toddler has been sleeping with you for 18 months, he is likely used to it. Now, you cannot just decide one fine day it needs to stop, and simply put him to sleep in his room. It doesn't work, and it will be a drastic change for your little one. The shock of it would prevent him from sleeping comfortably at night. Instead, start slowly. Talk to your little one about how he needs to sleep in his room. You could call it the "big kids" room and explain that he needs a room to himself *since he is a big kid.*

You can make the change easy by putting a positive spin on it. Don't forget to go through the soothing and consistent bedtime ritual every night. Ensure you set some time aside for cuddling and bonding with your little one. If you stick to this routine and encourage him to sleep in his room, he will soon get its hang. Don't forget to use the sleeping techniques and tips discussed in the previous sections. Another simple way to ensure that your child feels comfortable at night is by reassuring him that everything is okay and leaving the room. Even if he cries for a while, he will soon stop.

Sleep training takes time, effort, and patience. If one method doesn't work, try another approach.

Chapter Five: Potty Training Your Toddler

A major developmental milestone in your toddler's life is the end of using diapers and wipes. It might make your heart leap with infinite joy because your toddler has finally learned to stop "doing his business" in his diapers. Now, the next logical step you need to concentrate on is potty training him. This requires the consistent effort of all caregivers in your toddler's life. In this chapter, you will learn about identifying the signs your little one is ready to start potty training, positive parenting tips to make potty training more manageable, and how to overcome the common potty training problems you might face.

How to Start Potty Training

Signs of Readiness

Ideally, toddlers between the age of 18 and 24 months are often ready to be potty trained. However, there is no rush, and since every child grows at his own pace, don't worry even if he is three years old. If he takes a while longer to start, it is okay. No matter what age you start, here are signs of readiness you should watch out for.

One of the first signs of potty readiness is a dry diaper for over two hours. It essentially shows your little one's ability to hold it for a few hours. This is a positive sign, and don't forget to keep checking his diapers every two hours when he is between 18-24 months.

Another common sign is that your toddler seems interested in using the toilet: if he *likes* to sit on the potty, talks about using the potty, or is eager to use it, get started immediately. Toddlers are curious, and his readiness could be showcased by his curiosity of using the potty like grownups.

Around this stage, your toddler might also express a desire to go to the bathroom and can follow simple instructions you give him. If he can pull down or up the elastic of his underpants before or after going with no help, that's a readiness signal. If you notice he is reluctant to be potty trained, even after showing these signs, it isn't anything to worry about. It is okay to wait for a while longer and allow your child to be fully prepared for this step.

Other signs of readiness include regular bowel movements, any vocal expression about his wanting to go to the bathroom. If your toddler keeps happily broadcasting that time for him to pee or poop, encourage him to go to the toilet. Another sign: he no longer wants to stay in damp or dirty diapers.

Start Talking

If you are happy, cheerful, and enthusiastic about potty training, all these positive emotions will rub off on your little one. Therefore, always maintain a positive attitude while talking about potty training; be encouraging. Start the conversation about potty training by encouraging your little one to sit on the toilet, even when clothed. It helps build familiarity. You can also place some of his toys in the bathroom to make it seem less intimidating. It might not seem like much to an adult, but it is a major change for your little one. Therefore, try to view the situation from his perspective. Before you encourage him to sit on the potty, you can show how it's done by being fully clothed.

Another way to put a positive spin on this new change is by offering him choices, allowing him to feel more in control. It also reduces any struggles you might encounter . However, be mindful of the options you are offering. If you ask him a question like, "Do you want to use the toilet?" be prepared to receive "no," as an answer. Instead, you can ask him, "Do you want to wear your big kid underpants?" Or "Do you want to try on your new underpants?" It's likely he will be tempted to do these things.

If your little one looks scared, anxious, or resists no matter how much you try, take a break. You can attempt the training later. Unless he is ready, potty training will become an uphill battle.

He might also take an interest in seeing other kids his age using the bathroom - or even other adults. Use this technique only if you are 100% comfortable with it. For instance, you can casually lower your trousers and sit on the toilet and talk excitedly and animatedly about the process. Explaining the process and what you are feeling reduces any fear and uncertainty your little one might be feeling. If you love reading stories to your little one, you can both bond with him and encourage him with stories concerning potty training. It helps expose your child to characters experiencing the joys of this new step while entertaining at the same time.

Parents Need Help Too

Remember, it's not just your child who needs to be ready, even you should be consistent. You are your child's guide, and you need to be with him every step of the way. During the initial days, parents are excited and enthusiastic about the process and eagerly tend to their child and make sure he uses the bathroom regularly. However, when you get busy, you might tend to slide on this habit. Understand that every child develops at his own pace; some might get the hang of it right away, while others need more help.

If any other major changes happen in your toddler's life, wait for a while before potty training. Toddlers take a while longer to get used to change than adults do and process it differently. Some examples of big changes include welcoming a baby home, sleep training him, or moving to a new house.

During the initial stages, it is ideal to set a potty timer to remember it is time for your toddler to go. Ideally, set the timer for anywhere between 30 minutes-two hours, according to your child's needs. You can also use this technique to casually remind your child he is wearing "big kid underpants" and not his usual diapers. You could say something like, "You are wearing your big kid underpants and should use the toilet whenever you need to go." Ensure that your tone stays upbeat and excited while you talk about things related to potty training. Don't forget to get your toddler involved in this entire process. For instance, if you are using a timer to remind yourself, encourage your toddler to understand what it means when the timer goes off. Once it goes off, you could ask him, "What time is it?" The first couple of times, you need to answer the question yourself with an excited "It's potty time." After a couple of tries, your toddler will get the hang of it. Even if you don't hear the timer go off, he will remind you once it does.

It's not just using the toilet; you also need to teach him good personal hygiene. After he is done, don't forget to encourage him to wash his hands. This is one habit that will stay with him throughout his life.

Tips to Prepare Your Toddler for Potty Training

Your toddler might be ready to start potty training, but don't throw his diapers away, at least, not yet. Transitioning from diapers to using the toilet isn't simple! Consider the following tips.

Before you get started with potty training, motivate your child by stating the different benefits of using the toilet like an adult. For instance, you could say something like, "You are going to wear big-boy underwear" "New underwear is fun" or "You can start flushing just like mommy and daddy do!" However, be careful when using positive phrases for potty training. For instance, you should never mock your toddler's previous habits or make them seem babyish. If you do this, it will demotivate him and even make him resist the process.

Your toddler is growing, and if you acknowledge and appreciate his growth, it helps encourage positive behavior. Whenever you notice grownup behavior, such as drinking from his cup without spilling, willingly sharing his toys, or eating on his own, compliment or appreciate it. Don't expect any sophistication at this age. His behavior might not be as polished as an adult's behavior, but he is getting there. When he knows that you support his growth and development, his willingness to portray such behavior also increases. However, if you put too much pressure on him to start acting like a grownup, is it will prove regressive, and he may begin to miss the simple ways of his baby days.

You could also show him how to use the potty. Most behaviors and actions a toddler learns are mimicking those around him. You can explain a lot about squatting, doing his business, wiping, flushing, and washing hands, but it might not be as effective as show and tell. Instead of lecturing about all these things, show him what he needs to do. You could bring him with you to the bathroom and demonstrate. If you are uncomfortable doing this in front of him, you could demonstrate these actions while fully clothed. You can also use his favorite stuffed toy to explain the process.

Dress your toddler for potty training success, the pull-down and pull-up movements. If there are too many buttons or tricky hooks to remove, it complicates the process. Instead, choose stretchy clothes that can be easily pulled up and down. Encourage him to practice these maneuvers before potty training. Ask him to pull his pants down and pull them up. You can also make a game out of it by timing how long he takes to repeat these maneuvers. This makes it easier for him to repeat these maneuvers when it's time to go.

You need to slowly, but surely, bridge the gap between diapers and transitioning to using a toilet like an adult. The room where his potty is placed can be used to change his diapers. If you introduce the change in stages, it becomes easier to transition from using diapers to the toilet. After he soils his diaper, bring him to the washroom to see you flush the contents away. Don't be surprised if the flushing sound startles your little one. If he gets startled, simply dump it for now, and you could teach him about flushing later.

You also need a training potty. The design you choose should be strong, sturdy, and durable. If it is a flimsy structure, it might tip over when your child gets on it. To make things more exciting and increase your child's motivation to use the potty, you can go shopping for it. The more involved your child is in this process, the easier it is to potty train him. If he refuses to use the baby potty and wishes to use the adult toilet, you can purchase our potty seat, which could be attached to the toilet. If required, you might also need a small stool or footrest he can use to boost himself onto the toilet.

Tips to Get Started With Potty Training

Once you follow the different tips and suggestions in the previous section, it's time to get started. The previous steps helped lay down the groundwork required to successfully potty train your little one.

Instead of diapers, it's time to switch to pull-ups. During the initial stages, it would be ideal to choose disposable ones. The main advantage of using pull-ups is that he can easily pull them down like actual underpants - a helpful training tool. Also, even if he has an accident, the absorbent pull-up varieties will readily absorb his pee or poop and be easily removed. Once he gets the hang of using the toilet whenever he needs to go, you can shift to regular washable training pants.

During this stage, observe your little one closely. His body signals become apparent whenever he needs to go. If you pay attention to his cues, it becomes easier to train him and reduce any accidents. Some telltale signs of using the loo include straining or fidgeting. If you suspect he needs to use the toilet, you could ask him. If you were a little late in identifying the cues and already done the job, place him on the potty after lowering his underpants to establish the connection between the toilet and the urge to go.

You can also encourage your toddler to check for dryness as you used to when he was younger. It not only gives him a sense of control but also encourages self-confidence and self-esteem. It is a small task, but acknowledge and appreciate his effort. For instance, if he tells you he is dry, hug him, or pat him on the back. Let him know that he did something good, and you appreciate it. Positive reinforcement during potty training plays an enormous role. Likewise, don't lose your calm and patience if he has an accident.

To teach your toddler to learn of his body's signals, encourage him to bare his bottom. You can also let him walk around with a bare bottom in the yard or a room with washable floors. It becomes hard to ignore the pee or poop if there are no diapers or underpants to mask them. Also, ensure that his training potty is nearby if he needs to use it.

Ensure that you keep your toddler motivated during this stage. Keep gently reminding him it is a sign he is growing up. Whenever he uses the potty, tell him this is what all the big kids and adults too. Now that he is a big kid, he also needs to use the potty. During the initial stages, offering a small and tangible reward goes a long way. For instance, you could put a smiley sticker on his calendar whenever he uses the toilet. Or maybe put a penny in his piggybank when he does the deed. However, you need to slowly phase out the tangible rewards to prevent your little one from becoming dependent. You can replace it with praise and appreciation. After a while, this helps develop his inner motivation to use the toilet like grownups.

You need to remind him when he needs to go, but don't keep nagging him. If you constantly nag him, he probably will resist or stops telling you when he needs to go. Likewise, never force your toddler to keep sitting on the potty forcefully or for longer than required. If you force him to sit on the potty when he doesn't want to, even when you know he wants to go, it creates negative feelings toward using the toilet. Once this negative association takes root in his mind, undoing it becomes challenging.

Even if your toddler is enthusiastic about potty training, it can take a while before he gets the hang of it. Becoming proficient at it is not an overnight process and can take several weeks. Sometimes, it feels like you're taking one step forward and two steps back. This is common, and the only thing you need to remember is not to lose your patience. If you are loving, patient, and positive about the entire process, the journey becomes easier for you and your toddler. Also, don't set unrealistic expectations about the time required. Unrealistic expectations not only increase the stress on your toddler but also burden the relationship. Never punish, shame, or overreact if he has an accident. Do not these things if he doesn't want to use the toilet yet.

Never deny your toddler any drinks because you want to potty train him. You can reduce the number of fluids he consumes before bedtime, but not at other times. Even if he has an accident, remember to spin it positively. As to fluids, it's unfair and unhealthy to deny these; instead, steadily increase his intake of fluids, creating more teachable moments.

Positive Parenting and Potty Training

Don't Forget Your Manners

"Please," "thank you," and "sorry." Never forget these three golden words. All it takes is a little courtesy to get your toddler's attention. If you want him to use potty, use "please" in the sentence, so it doesn't seem like a command. However, do not say something that would prompt your toddler to say "no." For instance, you could tell him, "Please sit on the potty, and once you're done, we can go out and play." A sentence like this is not only courteous, but it also offers an incentive, which could act as an encouragement. Now, the toddler knows he needs to sit on the potty and do his job, and then it's time to play.

Don't Shame The Toddler

Never shame your toddler for his behavior. If he doesn't listen to you, change your approach, but don't belittle him. Embarrassing or reprimanding him is not effective, and it merely increases the chances of accidents. As adults, we don't like to be shamed, and the same logic applies to your toddler too. He is a little human. Do not admonish him if he has an accident or doesn't use the toilet as you asked him to; instead, offer loving and gentle guidance. Instead of reprimanding or shaming him, choose the effective approach of letting him know what you want him to do. For instance, you can get frustrated when he has an accident. Do not say things like, "Why didn't you tell me that you had an accident? Look at the mess you made." Such harsh sentences will effectively prevent him from trying in the future. Also, he might withdraw or regress. Instead, try saying something like, "The next time you need to go, let me know." In this way, you've not only offered him guidance, but have also shown him *what* you want him to do.

Using Praise

Using praise is a great way to motivate your little one for potty training. While you use praise, ensure it is specific and enthusiastic but does not place too much stress on a specific outcome. A simple form of praise could be a loving kiss or a hug, a pat on the back, or even a high-five. These gestures are encouraging and help your toddler feel confident. It also increases the chances of him repeating the same actions.

The praise you offer needs to be immediate and not given at a later stage. If he does something that makes you happy, tell him immediately. If you wait until later, he might not even remember the event.

Use praise but use it sparingly. Ensure it is used for a special occasion, and only when your toddler truly deserves it. This doesn't mean you should be stingy; it only means you need to choose the events wisely. If you keep praising him all the time, you will inadvertently turn your toddler into a praise junkie. The next time he does something, he will expect praise, and when he doesn't get what he thinks he deserves, he may feel upset and cranky.

Establish And Follow A Routine

Toddlers thrive when they have a routine. An established routine gives them a sense of security, but it also helps them understand what others expect of them. Therefore, it's important to establish a routine and stick to it consistently. Even if your child need not go, create a routine to teach him potty timings. For instance, as soon as he wakes up in the morning, gives him about five minutes, take him to the toilet, and sit him down on it. Likewise, ensure that you do the same after his mealtime, naps, and playtime. Once you have established a potty routine, ensure that everyone in the household follows it too.

Learn To Be Patient

Patience is a virtue, and it is critical in parenting. For anything associated with your little one, you need to be patient. Your toddler is new to this world, and he is slowly learning the ways of it and bound to make a few mistakes. Learn to keep your calm and don't take your frustration out on these little souls. If you notice that you both are constantly at loggerheads and your temper is flaring, step back and take a break. You can resume this activity after a week or two.

Support System

We all need a little support occasionally. You can rely on your pediatrician for support while potty training your little one. Besides this, you can talk to other parents, join online support forums, and chat rooms. When you know there are other parents experiencing this stage, you will feel infinitely better about your situation. When you talk to others, you might stumble across some advice you didn't think of before.

Countdown Calendar, And Sticker Charts

Treat stickers as rewards for whenever your child successfully uses the toilet. Place these little paper incentives on a chart in his bedroom, allowing him to place them himself whenever he uses the restroom to pee or poop.

You can also use a countdown calendar to begin the date when you want to start potty training. Ensure that you are upbeat about it and get your little one excited for potty training. For instance, if you wish to start potty training five days from now, mark the date on the calendar with a big x. Tell him it's an event you are excited for. As soon as you wake up your little one in the morning, tell him "5 days to go until you are a big boy!" the next day, it would be "4 days to go until you are a big boy," and so on. During this period, use a lot of positive talk about potty training. Tell him that big boys wear underpants and use the potty to do their business. Don't make it seem intimidating and keep things light and pleasant.

Overcome Potty Training Problems

This section will introduce you to a few other common potty training issues, and ways to overcome them.

Difference Between Pee And Poop

The toddler might understand that he needs to empty his bowels but doesn't recognize the urge to pee. Toddlers can take a while before they have complete control over their bladders. Meanwhile, there might be accidents that you need to prepare yourself for.

Squatting And Peeing

All toddlers - not just the girls - might be comfortable squatting and peeing instead of standing. If you notice your child doing this, don't worry. He might have observed his family members sitting down to pee, and he is doing the same. Once he grows older, he could learn how to stand and pee. This is up to him, and don't change this right now. The only thing you need to concentrate on is whether your toddler can *recognize his urge* to pee or empty his bowels.

A Little Too Curious

Toddlers are naturally curious, and this curiosity of theirs is healthy. Usually, it isn't anything you need to worry about. However, if your little one gets a little too curious and plays with his feces, it's time to intervene. You don't have to be stern or angry while intervening; this is common curiosity - he isn't acting out any ill ulterior motives. Therefore, carefully handle the situation. For instance, you could tell him, "This is not a toy," or "You should not play with this."

Dealing With Accidents

Dealing with accidents is an important part of potty training. Don't get upset when he has an accident; instead, treat it lightly, taking it in stride and moving right along. If you concentrate too much on it or make a big deal out of it, you will frighten, intimidate, embarrass, and belittle your little one!

Resists Pooping

If your child is resisting, he needs more time before he is ready for potty training. Whenever you notice he is about to pee or poop, take him to the potty area. Ensure that he is seated on it for a few minutes and no longer. Explain the process to him and tell him it's natural. Your words of encouragement and loving praise will give him the motivation required to be potty trained.

Scared Of The Toilet

Toddlers can fear the toilet itself. Yes, the big shiny white bowl that makes noises is a very intimidating object for a toddler. He could be scared of being sucked into it when he flushes. The sound of flushing could startle him. Both these things are common, and they can be easily overcome. For instance, you can stand with him on the site and encourage him to flush down toilet paper pieces. Once he realizes he has complete control over this object, the fear will likely resolve.

Flushed Away Poop

Don't be too surprised if you notice that your child is upset when he sees his poop being flushed away. Little children often believe their poop to be a natural part of the body instead of the waste it produces. Therefore, parting with it might be a scary instance for them. So, spend some time with your little one and explain that he need not hold onto the poop, and it is just his body eliminating the things it doesn't need.

Asks For Diapers

If you notice that your toddler is asking for diapers when he needs to have a bowel movement, but then goes to a special place to do this, it's a sign he isn't ready for potty training. He can recognize his physical urge to defecate but isn't mentally or emotionally ready for potty training. Don't think of it as an absolute failure. The first step of potty training is to teach your child to recognize these natural urges. Now that he recognizes it, it's okay to take some more time before you start potty training. So, keep a positive attitude and praise him for understanding when he needs to go.

Wrong Time

Sometimes, your toddler pees or poops after you remove him from the toilet (this usually happens right after you he leaves it.) It can be frustrating, but please, keep your calm. It also occurs during the early stages of potty training. It is a part of the process, and it will take your little one some time to understand how to relax the muscles in his bladder and bowel. Once he gains better control over these things, these accidents will happen less frequently. If this keeps happening and makes them uncomfortable, take a break from potty training; he isn't ready for this process.

Signs Of Regression

Stress can be a regressing factor. If your child is stressed, he will likely return to the previous level of development he is comfortable with. Shifting to a new house, illness, having guests at home, or even changing from sleeping in his crib to a bed could be stressful. If you notice he wants to use his diapers but has several accidents, it's time to stop potty training for a while. Give it a break, and you can start again after a few days. If you keep going while the child is stressed, it will prompt him to withdraw further and speed up the regression.

Comfort Level

Sometimes. toddlers are comfortable using the toilet only in the presence of certain individuals. This is normal, and to be expected. If you are the only one he is comfortable within the bathroom, don't worry. You need to withdraw yourself from the room gradually, and he will soon get used to doing the deed without help. For instance, you can offer to help him undress and walk away from the bathroom. You can reassure him by waiting outside and offer words of encouragement if required.

While potty training, prepare to deal with some bumps along the way, it will not be easy, but it is doable. By following the simple tips and suggestions discussed in this section, you can successfully potty train your toddler within a few weeks.

Chapter Six: Dealing with Tantrums and Misbehavior

Watching your little one grow is an incredible experience. From his first laugh to the first uncertain steps he takes and the words he utters, the journey is riddled with beautiful and unforgettable moments. However, certain things are not as pleasant, yet still a part of the growing up process. For instance, you might have heard about the terrible twos. Most parents dread this age. Are you wondering why? The period between 24-36 months is exciting for your toddler, and this is when they realize they are separate entities from the adults around them. Dealing with toddler tantrums is a part of a parent's job description, so be prepared.

This doesn't mean you need to accept all tantrums your toddler throws and don't correct his behavior. Dealing with tantrums and changing his behaviors for the better is an essential aspect of positive parenting. There are simple yet effective ways to deal with your toddler's tantrums without resorting to punishing him. Often, parents scream and shout at their toddlers while they are throwing tantrums. Before you do this, it's important to understand *why* he is throwing a tantrum, and what you can do to fix it? Once you have the answers to these questions, maintaining peace at home becomes easier, and it also helps your toddler deal with his emotions, reducing the chances of undesirable behavior.

Why Do Toddlers Misbehave?

A common question many parents fail to answer or even think about is *why* their toddlers misbehave.

Visualize this scenario. Your two-year-old kid starts screaming at the grocery store, saying, "Mommy, I just want candy!" You tell him to calm down and that he cannot have a candy bar. Before you even realize what's happening, he is screaming, shouting, and crying like there's no tomorrow. You look at him aghast, trying to understand what happened while everyone at the store is staring. Your tiny toddler has now become the center of attention, and you are utterly baffled. This is a common scenario that we've probably all watched play out. Don't think of it as a failure on your part as a parent, but it's time to consider why your toddler is misbehaving.

All the crying, screaming, shouting, whining, and kicking are a part of toddler's tantrums. These are perhaps the only ways the little ones can communicate with the adults around them. Remember, your child hasn't yet learned how to effectively communicate what he or she is feeling. At two or three years old, toddlers begin to assert themselves and are inclined to communicate their likes and dislikes. They also try to act as independently as they can. During this period, toddlers are also learning to communicate and develop their communication skills to express what they want or need, or their ideas. It is a period of growth, but the toddler is still too young to understand the logic and has a hard time understanding the concept of self-control and patience. So, even seemingly harmless words such as "no," or "don't" can set him off.

In this age group, toddlers are learning to handle their strong emotions. Even adults have a tough time managing their big emotions; can you imagine how overwhelming it would be for a toddler? For instance, we have the luxury of explaining what we're feeling and the reasons for the same. However, a toddler is still learning to do all these things. If he cries or throws a tantrum, it's probably because it's the only way he knows to communicate. It doesn't mean tantrums are acceptable. However, understanding the reasons he is acting out is a starting point.

Do not jump to the conclusion that your toddler is a brat because he throws tantrums. Babies have absolutely no awareness about anything at the time of birth. As they grow, they learn new things. On the other hand, a two-year-old might have learned to walk. He probably wants to explore the world, is learning and fine-tuning his motor skills, and has picked up vocabulary. Armed with all this, the toddler would look for opportunities to improve these skills and use them.

So, what seems to be the problem? While doing all this, toddlers look to their parents for support, safety, comfort, and encouragement. A toddler might be proud of his artwork. However, the parent might be upset upon discovering that the canvas for their toddler's artwork is the freshly painted wall in the living room. He might try to stand on his highchair, while the parent removes him and places him on the floor. A parent does these things trying to protect their toddler, who might feel frustrated that instead of encouragement, all his efforts are met with "No," "Stop!" "Don't do that!" and so on. As a parent, you might not realize it, but all these things trigger disappointment, anger, frustration, and a lot of internal turmoil. Essentially your toddler is dealing with a bunch of foreign emotions and isn't coping well. If your toddler throws a temper tantrum, think of it as an outlet for his strong emotions.

If your toddler has a meltdown down because you don't understand his words, says yes when he means no, gets upset, throws his toys around, doesn't like settling for substitutes, and acts out when frustrated, it means he is struggling to cope with his emotions. He is also learning to assert his independence. It essentially means he is trying to do more things on his own but gets upset or frustrated when he cannot do it or is prevented from doing it. For instance, don't be surprised if your toddler screams and shouts when you try feeding him because he is making a mess while eating. What do you think went wrong? As a parent, you are probably trying to help him eat. From a toddler's perspective, you are taking away his independence. The reasons for toddler's tantrums are often simple and obvious. All it takes is a little patience to understand it. Once you understand the reason, tackling it and preventing such meltdowns becomes easier.

Even science backs these claims. Whenever your toddler is overcome by a powerful emotion such as anger, frustration, or disappointment, his amygdala (part of the brain), the center of emotional responses, is triggered. This releases a burst of stress hormones that further intensify the toddler's emotions. The anguish it unleashes in the form of emotional discord is like physical anguish one might experience. Unless the brain's prefrontal cortex is developed - the region that regulates strong emotions - the child cannot fully control himself. This region is still in the developing stages, and therefore, toddlers throw tantrums.

Another aspect of brain biology that needs to be considered: the brain's thinking area isn't fully mature until the individual is in their mid-20s. This is another reason that not only toddlers, but even older kids have trouble regulating their emotions. Toddlers between the ages of three and five can have such tantrums, as they are just an outlet for emotions. Once you teach your little one to regulate his emotions, the tantrums will eventually resolve.

There are billions of neurons present in the brain at birth. These neurons need to be connected to facilitate rational and logical thinking. However, babies have only a few neural connections (or "synapses.") Synapses help regulate emotions and facilitate thinking, reasoning, and decision-making, and are *only developed through life experiences.* Understanding and regulating one's emotions during a temper tantrum or an outburst helps establish the much-needed synaptic connections. If your toddler learns the right way to handle his emotions without getting overwhelmed, the neural pathways developed in his young brain will stay with him as he grows.

Once he learns to manage his options and stress, it becomes easier for him to become assertive and independent later in life. If he isn't given the right opportunities or is denied a chance to regulate his emotions, it will harm his emotional and mental development. For instance, if you punish your toddler for having an outburst or throwing a tantrum, it prevents him from learning how to handle stress and other emotions. The child might internalize his feelings and suppressing certain emotions, which can later cause severe emotional and mental trouble. It's not just internalization of problematic issues; externalizing it through aggressive behavior or substance abuse later in life is undesirable. This is one reason childhood years are considered the formative years of a person's life. Therefore, it's quintessential that parents deal with their little one's outbursts and tantrums without doling out punishment.

Dealing with Toddler Tantrums

Now that you understand the reasons for a toddler's tantrums and the brain chemistry at work, let's look at simple tips to deal with them.

Don't Try To Reason

A common mistake parents make while dealing with their toddler's outburst is trying to reason with the child. You cannot reason with your toddler during a tantrum. Your toddler will neither understand, much less listen to, logical reasoning. Instead of getting frustrated in this, take a break. Don't engage with him but *do* remove him from any situation that might harm him. Allow the tantrum to run its course, and there will be plenty of time for explanations later. Your toddler is in no state of mind to listen to anything you say. So, save your breath and prevent the situation from escalating by disengaging.

Offer A Distraction

A toddler's attention span is limited; he's easily distracted. You can effectively use this to your advantage. If your toddler is upset because he cannot go out and play, offer a distraction by asking him if he would want to play with his favorite toy. Your offer should be something you can live with. Don't offer distractions as a form of emotional resolution. Instead, think of it as a means to calm your toddler.

Staying Calm And Positive

It is easy to lose your cool or get upset when your toddler throws a tantrum. If everyone in the room were shouting and screaming, would it help? No, that merely escalates the situation. To avoid this, stay calm, composed, and positive. Your toddler is sensitive to your emotions and vibes. If you get upset, it merely intensifies the emotions he feels, which triggered the tantrum. It will do you good to remember you are the adult and you must act like one. Staying calm and positive differs from giving in. You don't have to smile, but don't frown or look disappointed.

Restore And Emotional Balance

A toddler's emotional brain is like the gas pedal of a car, and the thinking brain is the brake. Living through toddlerhood is like driving with no brakes. Now, a tantrum is a runaway car. To disengage such behavior, you can offer a hug. The physical act of lovingly hugging your toddler during a tantrum is like disengaging the transmission in the runaway car without brakes. Don't wrongly believe that giving a hug is a reward for his behavior. Instead, think of it as a tool to disengage the transmission system.

The next time your toddler cries, screams, kicks, and flails his arms, try hugging him. This physical gesture prevents him from acting out or harming himself accidentally. Communicate the simple message, "You are loved, and I understand you." Never underestimate the power of hugging; it works.

Don't Use Punishment

Never punish your toddler for having a tantrum. If you punish him when he acts out, he will believe he shouldn't express his emotions and may suppress them instead. Visualize this scenario: you are in a lot of pain to the extent that you start writhing on the floor. If your loved one shouts or punishes you for expressing your pain, how would you feel? Chances are, you will feel more miserable than you did before. Also, what is the message you'll receive? You probably feel that others don't care about you and are inconsiderate of your feelings. The next time your toddler is throwing a tantrum, remind yourself of this scenario. A principle of positive parenting is to view the situations from your toddler's perspective instead of yourself. Every situation can be viewed from multiple perspectives. By changing your perspective, you get a better understanding of what your toddler must be feeling.

Therefore, don't punish him for acting out. Instead, gently correct his behavior later. If you believe a tantrum will not end soon and intervention is required, give him time in. Time-in differs from a timeout. In a time-in, you are physically shifting your toddler from the environment that triggered the tantrum to a calm and peaceful place. Sit with him during this period, and just be there. He will calm down, and once he is calm, you can talk to him again.

Teach Emotional Vocabulary

Toddlers often throw tantrums because they cannot deal with all the emotions they feel and experience. By teaching him emotional vocabulary or improving his communication skills, you can reduce tantrums. Even if you cannot immediately reduce the number of such incidents, it will teach him to manage the situation better. Don't try teach him vocabulary for better self-expression during the tantrum; instead, allow him to calm down and let the emotional tornado settle. For instance, if your toddler threw a tantrum because he was denied something, you can explain different ways he could better express himself the next time.

After he calms down, you can narrate the circumstances that led to the tantrum and how he behaved. Using simple words to explain this to your child helps develop important neural connections required for managing emotional situations. You can also try and explain how you feel whenever he throws a tantrum. For instance, you can say, "I feel sad when you throw a tantrum."

Simple feelings such as anger, sadness, happiness, excitement, and upset can be taught. You can also use imaginary characters and his favorite stuffed toys to explain all this. For instance, you could tickle him, and when you both laugh, you could say it means to be this happy. Likewise, if someone cries, it means they are sad. By teaching him these simple words, you enhance its ability to deal with his emotions while expressing his needs.

Prevent A Tantrum

Prevention is always better than cure the same stands true for tantrums too. Here's a simple acronym you can use to prevent a tantrum or reduce their occurrences. The acronym is HALT, and it stands for hunger, anger, loneliness, and tiredness. There are certain physical factors such as tiredness and hunger that can trigger a tantrum. It's not just toddlers, and even adults tend to get a little cranky when they are hungry or tired. Even if just one of the physical factors discussed in the acronym occurs, it acts as a trigger. The simplest way to avoid all these things is by establishing a proper bedtime routine for your child to get his good night's sleep. Ensure that your child is well-fed and has his meals and snacks on time. If you realize he has agitated, for no apparent reason, you could offer him a snack. Other triggers such as boredom, stress, disappointment, frustration, and anger can also effectively trigger tantrums.

As an example, if you know your child will be disappointed if you don't take him to the zoo as promised, be sure to have an alternative in mind. When that moment comes, offer an equally good distraction. Maybe you can go to the park, play his favorite game, or watch a movie together.

All the tips in this section are based on the simple concepts of positive parenting. Don't use these tips only during a tantrum; use some for preventing it in the first place! If you teach your child about emotions and communicating them, it becomes easier to understand what he needs. It also helps the child calm down when he knows he is understood.

Chapter Seven: Encouraging Creativity And Imagination

Toddlers are creative and imaginative. They might lack logical thinking and reasoning, and they make up for it with their creativity and imagination. As your toddler's primary caregiver, encourage him to develop and explore the potential of his creativity, remembering that this gift is also crucial for problem-solving. In the previous chapter, we talked about the prefrontal cortex being in the developing phase during toddlerhood. The more he exercises his mental muscles, the stronger they become. This section provides simple games and activities for your toddler to enhance his creativity and imagination.

By the time your toddler is 24-months old, his creativity and imagination will develop in full swing. It's likely very entertaining and amusing to watch him unleash these characteristics. He might plop a blob of paint on a piece of paper and call it a cat or wave a straw and pretend he's a knight! He could probably tell you he plans on visiting the moon with such conviction it puts a smile on your face.

Toddlers might not understand logic or rational thinking, but they certainly make up for all this in imagination. For learning, imagination is a powerful tool that can improve his overall skills. You can improve your child's social, verbal, and thinking skills by engaging in pretend plays. You can narrate scenarios, read stories together, or act out characters from his favorite cartoons using his toys to create "shows" together. A great thing about encouraging your toddler's creativity is that it's the first step towards teaching him problem-solving skills. Unless he can think outside the box, dealing with obstacles in life can become a little overwhelming.

Exploring his imagination and creativity also gives him a chance to understand what the grown-up world is like. His artistic inclinations can fine-tune his motor skills while playtime can teach him the importance of teams. All these things give him the tools to express his emotions and feelings. Unless given an opportunity, a child cannot explore his potential. This is where parents need to step in and help their little one explore!

During toddlerhood, a primary goal is encouraging your child's creativity and imagination. It doesn't matter whether he wishes to pursue these talents later; this helps prepare his mind to answer questions, solve problems, and makes him more mentally agile. The mind is also a muscle, and the body exercises, the stronger it becomes. You need no expensive supplies or toys to teach all these things. All it takes is genuine interest and praise to increase his creativity. Even simple props such as crayons, colorful markers, papers, and water will come in handy. It's not just your child who will enjoy this – you can too. Whenever you engage in playtime together, it gives you a chance to bond with him. This bond will stay with him forever, and it is something he will come to enjoy and look forward to. You are helping your child grow and learn and equipping him with important life skills.

Here are simple ways to encourage your child to explore his creative side and allow his imagination to run wild.

Spend more time playing with your little one. Whenever you play, ensure you always follow his lead and let him believe he is the leader. Whether he is the knight in shiny armor fighting off the evil dragon or flying to the moon in his cardboard "rocket," he simply follows what he's doing. Be as encouraging as you can during this period. Let him come up with a story, and maybe you can pitch in and offer ideas. Avoid the temptation of interjecting and guiding him on how he's supposed to do things. This creative interaction and support will help your child grow.

Another great way to engage him is by participating in household chores together as a team. It can be painting a room or putting away the groceries. Simple household activities are a great bonding idea. It also allows you to teach him problem-solving skills without depending on others. For instance, if a room needs to be painted, you can paint it together. Don't expect any perfection from him, but he would undoubtedly enjoy painting a wall; after all, it is a big canvas.

Sometimes, your child will seek your help or assistance with something he is doing. The answer might be simple, and you will be tempted to do it for him. Instead, step back and let him explore the different options available. You can also talk about the problem to prompt him to come up with suggestions and ideas. Allow him to implement these ideas and see for himself whether they work. If he cannot complete the task, you can step in and tell him what he can do. Don't complete the task for him but do let him implement your idea. If he comes up with some ideas and suggestions, offer praise and encouragement. However, do not go overboard with the praise, or he'll soon get used to excessive praise, which is problematic.

We live in a world dominated by devices. A simple way to encourage your child to explore his creativity is by teaching him photography. You can give him your smartphone or tablet and teach him how to click, save, and edit pictures. Once he gets the hang of it, set a time limit and let him explore the surroundings. If he takes any good pictures, tell him he did a fantastic job. You can also teach him how he can improve upon his photography skills.

Another way to encourage your child's creative thinking and imagination is by giving him a scenario and asking him to visualize how it will be. For instance, you can ask him what he would do if he were a character in his favorite cartoon or if he had superpowers. You can ask him, "What would you do if you were Superman for a day?" Patiently await his replies and prepare to be surprised. When you do this, don't ridicule his answers and ideas. Instead, join in and tell him what you would want to do.

Children love going out with their parents. The next time you visit the local museum or the zoo, talk to your child about it before the outing. Spend some time and tell him the different things he could experience there and expect to see. For instance, if you are going to the zoo over the weekend, tell him about different animals. When you go to the zoo, you can point out these animals and prompt him to recollect the different things you shared with him. This is also a great way to excite him about the outing.

Playing with water is fun. You can teach him how to make bubbles with a homemade soap solution. Children love bubbles! Give him a straw, show him how to blow bubbles, and start with your fun playtime. You can also teach him about light and rainbows using a garden hose. You need only to pick a date when the sun is shining bright in the sky. Go to the garden or the yard, pick up the garden hose, and put it on the mist setting. If you don't have a hose, you can use a spray can to spray in an area that catches direct sunlight. Once the natural light hits the stream of water or mist, a rainbow will be formed due to the refraction of light. He might be too young to understand what refraction means, but he will enjoy the rainbows he's making.

The next time it rains, let him play in the rain. Dress him up in his raincoat and boots, give him an umbrella, and let him have fun. It is okay if he gets dirty while stomping or rolling around in the mud. It is all right for him to enjoy spending time in nature. It will make him feel happy, and all the smiles and giggles will be worth cleaning up the mess.

Try cooking or baking together. If he loves chocolate chip cookies, try baking a batch along with him! Involve him in this activity, and he will love spending time with you. It also teaches him a little about cooking.

If there is a simple family problem, allow your child to come up with solutions for it. For instance, if the dining area is often dirty or at the living room is cluttered, ask him what can be done. It's not just the adults who can solve problems; even children can pitch in. For instance, if the question is, "What can we do about the messy living room?" He would probably say it needs to be cleaned regularly, or certain items need to be removed. If he gives you any suggestions, tell you to appreciate his inputs and see if it can be implemented. After he gives the suggestions, encourage him to help you implement them.

Another way to increase his creative thinking is by asking him simple questions. "What is the one toy you would want every child in the world to have?" Or "If you could get one gift every day, what would you want?" The idea is not to give him gifts or toys, but about letting him think about what he wants.

The next time you go grocery shopping, take your little one with you. Allow him to identify the different fruits, vegetables, and any other ingredients he knows. For instance, if his favorite fruit is an apple, allow him to pick up apples at the grocery store.

Go out for brief evening walks. Let him gather pebbles, rocks, twigs, flowers, etc., on his walks. Once you are home, you can sit together and make up a story about all the items you found. You can make a scrapbook and write about the different items he picked up. If he finds a shiny pebble, you both could conjure up a story it was left by an imaginary character!

Encourage your child to choose his clothes. It is a straightforward activity, but it prompts him to think about different colors, patterns, and combinations. If he puts together a new combination, ask him to wear it and ask him for his opinion. If he likes it, take a picture of it and put it in his room. If he doesn't like it, ask him what he would change about it.

If your child does something that makes him feel bad, don't tell him it doesn't matter. Instead, ask him why he is bothered by it, and how he can improve himself. By making him think independently, it increases his self-confidence. Once he identifies a reason and believes it is the right reason, praise him and congratulate his efforts.

While you follow all the tips discussed in this section, there are a few things you should never do – never interfere and don't take over. You can offer guidance, but that's all you're supposed to do. If your child is making a mistake, allow him to. Experience is an excellent teacher, and he will learn from his experiences. If your child does nothing to hurt himself physically, don't interfere. When you allow him to make his own decisions, it inspires a sense of confidence and independence.

Chapter Eight: Building Self-Esteem And Confidence

Most toddlers are inherently confident and surprisingly independent. As they grow and explore the world, their traits develop too. However, not all toddlers need to be confident and independent. Some can lie on the other end of the spectrum too. No two toddlers are the same. They all develop at their own pace. Don't be worried if your little one doesn't seem as confident as you would want him to be. There are different tips and strategies to develop his confidence levels. Yes, it is not just adults who could use a little help with these things; even toddlers need some assistance.

Self-esteem is how one sees his value in the world, while confidence is the belief in one's abilities to do things. These two concepts are interrelated. If your child is not confident, he might seem withdrawn, disinterested, and shy. The same behavior shows up if his self-esteem is a little low. The good news is you can help increase these two things in your little one. The sooner you start, the better it is. Here are tips that will come in handy.

Tips to Build Self-Confidence

Validation

It's a natural tendency to seek validation, and your toddler is no different. Therefore, be mindful that you validate his feelings and don't write them off. If he is a little shy, accept it, and validate his behavior. If you don't validate his feelings, you are prompting him to withdraw even further. When you talk about it, it allows you to talk about emotions and how he can handle them also. For instance, if you notice he is shy whenever he meets new people or goes to new places, acknowledge his feelings. You could say something like, "I understand you feel a little shy whenever we go to new places." After this, don't forget to reassure him it is okay to feel shy, but there are ways to deal with it. You could also tell him you feel shy at times, and how you deal with that.

No Labeling

Don't label your child as shy or nervous. Once you label him, the label itself becomes self-fulfilling. Also, these labels have a habit of sticking and making your child question and second-guess himself every step of the way. If you keep calling him shy, it's likely he will behave shyly. A better way to tell him this is by saying, "It is okay to feel shy." Instead of saying he is shy, you are sharing about a specific emotion.

Acknowledgment

If you notice your little one is doing something new or attempting something for the first time, don't forget to praise his efforts instead of concentrating on the results. If he realizes the effort counts, his willingness to make an effort increases. It also takes away the fear of failure. Yes, even children feel this. If you know that he often feels shy at new places, but he's willingly talking to someone, praise his effort. Tell him you appreciate what he's doing. Positive reinforcement is a great way to teach him what good behavior is. The praise he receives from you will act as an incentive.

Role Model

Since children learn by copying the behavior of those around them, it's time to start role-modeling good behavior. Show him how to be confident and resilient. Even when you feel unsure or frustrated because of something, stick to it, and ensure it reaches a logical conclusion. This is a great way of showing your little one how to be resilient. For instance, if you are frustrated with a project at work, don't give up. Instead, try to deal with it to the best of your abilities.

A Little Preparation

Low confidence can also stem from uncertainties about the future. Since the future is uncertain and you cannot predict it, the best way to remove this uncertainty is via preparation. If you are introducing him to a new activity, prepare him for it. Tell him about it, explain what's to be done, and show him the benefits it offers. For instance, if you need to take your toddler to a birthday party, tell him what he can expect. Once he knows what he can expect and the situation he will be in, he will be better equipped to deal with it.

Unconditional Love And Acceptance

Babies share a strong emotional attachment with their primary caregivers. This bond never goes away, and it doesn't weaken as they grow. They depend on you for love, safety, security, and support. If you show him he is loved and accepted unconditionally, the way he is with no terms or conditions; it instills confidence. It also shows he will be loved and appreciated regardless of whatever happens. Never underestimate the power of a genuine hug, a pat on the back, or even a kiss. It essentially conveys the feeling is that he is a worthy human, and he can be loved the way he is. If you show your love and acceptance only when he does something good, he will believe he needs to be perfect to attain such love and praise. Don't do this. Eventually, it creates undesirable behaviors and attitudes in the child – and more importantly, in the adult he grows into.

Encouragement

As with love and acceptance, even encouragement matters a lot. When you encourage your little one's ability to solve problems, it improves his self-confidence. Give him a few problems you know he can solve and allow him to solve them. Once he solves the problem, offer some praise and incentives. It could be something as simple as putting together a puzzle or learning a new game. If he does these things successfully, encourage him. Once he can complete things on his own, it instills a sense of confidence and independence.

Know Your Limits

Offering encouragement is important, and you should encourage him to deal with new situations in life. However, don't push him too hard. Similarly, you shouldn't be overprotective. Learn to be sensitive about how to encourage him and don't cross such limits. If it is something he isn't ready to do yet, don't force him. If you go overboard, you are encouraging him to withdraw himself even more. For instance, if you know he feels uncomfortable in new situations, don't send him to preschool without preparation. Instead, do these things slowly. When the change is gradual, his ability to adapt to it increases. Likewise, don't be overprotective and don't prevent him from trying out new things. Children tend to lack confidence when their parents are overprotective. If you keep doing everything for him, he will never learn how to be independent. The lack of independence will harm his confidence too.

Decision Time

By giving your toddler a chance to decide, you give him a chance to improve his confidence. It can be something as simple as deciding the clothes he wants to wear the food he wants to eat. Even if the clothes don't make sense together, let him decide. Once he sees how the clothes look on him, he might want to change his mind. When he knows he can decide for himself, it gives him a sense of control, which improves his confidence.

Ability To Say No

Allow your little one to say no. When he says no, learn to respect it. It doesn't mean you listen to him every time he says "no" to the different things you say. Instead, it merely means he should be allowed to a certain what he wants and doesn't want to do in certain situations. For instance, if your toddler fusses that he wants to wear sandals when it's cold outside, restrain yourself from saying no. Tell him, "You will feel cold if you wear your sandals today." After this, let him do it. While learning the consequences of his actions, he will become more confident. Create situations where "no" is a perfectly acceptable answer.

One Step At A Time

Whenever it comes to new situations, ensure that you split it into smaller steps for your little one while boosting his confidence. A major change can be scary for him. If he cannot get adjusted to such a change, it will hurt his confidence. Therefore, take things one step at a time. For instance, if he needs to start preschool, start slowly. You can visit the preschool, spend some time there, and maybe attend a class with him. Gradually, he will be comfortable on his own, and it isn't anything to worry about. Also, when he spends more time with kids his age, his confidence will improve.

Tips to Build Self-Esteem

One of the best gifts you can give your child is a positive sense of self. Self-esteem is also important if you want him to develop into a happy and productive individual. In this section, let's look at simple tips to enhance its overall sense of self.

In the earlier chapters, we talked about why it's important to give your child choices. Ensure the choices give are well within reason and acceptable alternatives to one another. When you give him choices and let him choose, it makes him feel empowered and in control. He also learns that he's in control of his actions *and subsequent consequences*. This is a great way to teach him how to make simple choices in life.

Never offer any insincere praise and unnecessary compliments. Praise your child's efforts when truly needed. Instead of concentrating on the results, praise him for his efforts. However, the praise should be genuine and necessary. For instance, don't gush that he is the next Picasso when he paints something. Instead, you can say, "I appreciate your effort," or "You can be a god at it with a little practice." By doing this, you praise the effort that goes into the process, instead of offering insincere compliments.

Another great way to build self-esteem is by giving him age-appropriate responsibilities. Simple responsibilities for a toddler include putting his toys away, helping you arrange the dining table, or even selecting his clothes. You will learn more about different age-appropriate chores in the next chapter. When you give him some responsibilities around the house, it makes him feel like a valued and contributing member of the household. This simple feeling goes a long way in instilling self-esteem.

Restrain yourself from calling your child names, labeling him, or using sarcastic remarks to make a point. If he does something wrong, tell him what he did wasn't right, and show him how to do it properly. Don't call him any names or say things like, "This is stupid," or "How silly of you." Statements like this can sting and will slowly eat away at his self-esteem and confidence. You don't have to like everything your child does, but there is a proper way of showing your displeasure.

Most of us are guilty of drawing comparisons. Avoid comparing your child with those around him. If you keep comparing him with others, it will make him feel devalued, and you are essentially belittling him. He will question his self-worth, and it will erode his self-esteem and confidence. Remember, every child is different, and everyone grows at his own pace.

Ensure that you follow the advice in this section consciously and consistently. You cannot increase your child's self-esteem or confidence overnight. These personality traits are often a culmination of a variety of small events. Whenever your toddler completes a task or does something without being asked, it increases his sense of self-worth and confidence. A recurrence of such feelings over a period will enhance his overall sense of self-esteem, confidence, and independence.

Chapter Nine: Forming Positive Daily Habits

Habits aren't formed overnight. It is an ongoing process. If you keep doing a specific activity repeatedly at a given time, you develop a habit. The key to developing good habits is to start young. Work with your toddler and help him form good habits. An important aspect of doing this is to do it daily.

Positive Discipline for a Peaceful Home

Maintaining peace at home is quintessential for all family members. Constant power struggles and tantrums will disrupt this peace. The best way to reduce the risk of any unpleasantness at home is by establishing a routine for your little one. You will learn more about it in the subsequent sections. Now, let's look at simple ways to use positive discipline to create a happy and peaceful home environment.

Offer Information

Toddlers usually act out because it's the only way they know how to deal with the situation. They still don't know how to process, handle, and express themselves effectively. They are learning, and you need to be patient. A great way to speed up this process is by offering a lot of information to help them cope with the situation. If you notice your little one is acting out, provide information. Providing information isn't about questioning him, teaching him a lesson, or fixing the situation. It's merely just sharing things. For instance, if you notice your toddler is getting cranky because he cannot wear his nightclothes, tell him, "I realize you are getting frustrated that you cannot wear your pajamas properly." Or you might tell him, "I could help you, but you don't want me to. Why don't you try wearing them the other way and see?" By calmly providing information, you are offering him a choice. When you give him this information, you are essentially trying to understand his side of the story. Once he gets the information he needs, he'll be more pliable to listening to your direction.

Boundaries Matter

Boundaries matter a lot, and they are like safe walls that keep unnecessary things away from you. Remember, your toddler is still in the learning stage of understanding how to deal with frustration and boundaries. He is working on improving his confidence and self-control. If your toddler throws a tantrum or engages in a power struggle with you, it means you need to make more effort to teach him how to cope with the strong emotions he feels instead of doing away with your boundaries.

For instance, your toddler might throw a tantrum when you serve juice in a different sippy cup. Before every meal, give him two choices wherein he gets to choose the sippy cup he wants to drink from. Once he's chosen it, serve his beverage in that sippy cup. If he wants to change or use another sippy cup, tell him he needs to wait until the next meal is served. It teaches him patience and helps him deal with any frustration he feels. No matter what might have triggered the tantrum, step back and offer information.

Imagine the scenario. You splurge $ 300 on a new bag, go home, and realize it is not the bag you wanted, and now you wish to return it. However, the store has no return policy. It will make you feel frustrated and angry. These are the same things your toddler experiences when he feels powerless and helpless. By giving him choices and some information, you make him feel more in control.

Boundary Testing Is Common

Toddlers are curious, and a great way for them to learn is by testing the boundaries of those around them. If he's throwing a tantrum or is shouting, use every iota of self-control you must keep your calm. Losing your temper right now will not do either of you any favors. Instead of allowing your emotions to get the better of you, take control. Remember, the boundaries you have are your own. No one can invade them. Toddlers will test your boundaries. Just because he's testing your boundaries, it doesn't mean you give in. Stick to them without invalidating your child's emotions.

Physical Boundaries Matter Too

A lot of parents wrongly believe that physical boundaries cannot be used peacefully. Well, this is nothing more than a myth. If you realize your child will harm himself or someone around, it's okay to implement physical boundaries. For instance, if your toddler raises his hand to hit his sibling or another child, you can gently grab his arm to prevent him from hitting others. If you notice he's trying to climb on top of the kitchen counter, put your hand out to prevent him from doing this. Physical boundaries are important. If you see that your toddler repeatedly gets up from the bed after you tuck them in for the night, gently guide him back to the bed. These are simple examples, but they are effective and important to safety and health. This is so much better than indulging in any verbal power struggles with him. It's not only gentle, but it also doesn't undermine your little one's confidence. Try to keep it at a minimum, and always do it lovingly, peacefully, and gently.

Chores for Toddlers

The importance of creating a routine for toddlers has been repeatedly stressed in this book. A routine isn't just about encouraging him to wake up, brush, or sleep at specific times.

Instead, it is about creating different tasks the toddler can do during the day. It is quintessential the tasks should be age-appropriate. For instance, expecting the toddler to do laundry or cut vegetables will merely set you and your tiny tot up for disappointment. While thinking about different chores your toddler can do, you merely need to simplify the regular chores adults do and make it age-appropriate. Since we are talking about creating a routine, the tasks you give him must become a part of his daily activities.

Once you make these tasks or chores a part of his routine, he will do them automatically, such as brushing his teeth. If your toddler refuses to do the task when you ask him to, you can try it together. Chances are your toddler will be excited to be assigned additional responsibilities around the house. After all, he sees his parents and other caregivers perform a variety of activities daily. Now that he has certain responsibilities, it will make him feel like an adult too. This is one thing that all children crave, regardless of their age; they all want to be treated as adults. By teaching him responsibilities, you show him that certain chores and tasks are a part of that responsibility.

In this section, let's look at some simple tasks to encourage your little one. Remember, you might have to teach him how the task should be performed a couple of times before he gets the hang of it. Before leaving it entirely up to him, do trial runs well; you both perform the tasks together. This is a great bonding technique too.

Tidying The Room

Encourage him to put his toys away after playtime. Show him how to put his toys away and ask him to repeat your actions. Fix a dedicated space for all his toys and encourage him to put them away in their designated spot. This simple task goes a long way while parenting and managing the household.

Putting Clothes Away

A simple chore you can get your little one involved in is putting his clothes away. Encourage him to put his dirty clothes in the laundry basket.

Cleaning Up After Meals

You can ask your toddler to carry his cup, bowl, plate, or even utensils to the dishwasher after a meal. He will probably hand them to you since he cannot reach the dishwasher.

Make The Bed

Another simple task you can give the toddler is to show him how to make his bed after waking up. He will not have the skills required to make stiff corners or fold the blanket, but he can help rearrange his soft toys and fluff the pillows. When you and your little one work together, it gives you a chance to teach him ideal behavior while strengthening the bond you share.

Putting Away Clean Laundry

After you fold the fresh and clean clothes, you can ask your toddler to help you carry them. You can give him a single item of clothing or two at the most. He need not place them in the dresser drawers, but he can help carry them there.

Putting Away Groceries

As soon as you get groceries home, ask your tiny tot for a little assistance. From washing vegetables to placing them in the refrigerator, these are little ways he can contribute.

Your toddler will be happy to tackle these chores with you. This is what big kids do, and you could excite him about doing these chores by telling him the same. While you give him a task, don't rush into it. Allow him to explore everything at his own pace. He is still learning the ways of the world. Whenever you notice he has completed the task, don't forget to praise him. If you catch him doing the task on his own with no reminder, offer praise. Don't go overboard with a preview offer, but don't be stingy with it either. When he knows he's doing something that you appreciate, it helps reinforce is positive behavior.

When you give him certain responsibilities around the home and give him the freedom to perform them as he sees fit, it helps increase his overall confidence levels. His self-esteem also increases. When his positive behavior is reinforced, his willingness to complete the tasks increases, he can take a while until he gets the hang of it. In the meanwhile, you need to be patient. Don't forget to teach him how to do the activity before assigning the responsibility. If he makes any mistakes, gently and lovingly correct him without chiding or shaming him. If he asks you about the activity, indulge him, and don't get irritated.

Besides the activities discussed in this section, there are several other chores where your toddler can participate. From removing weeds in the garden to dusting or mopping, setting up the table, wiping down the table, emptying the dishwasher, cleaning vegetables, and so on, there are many ways he can become an active member of the household. By encouraging him to actively participate in household activities, you are teaching him self-reliance and independence from a young age. These two traits go a long way in the real world, and it's a great way to ensure your toddler's overall development.

One simple thing you should never forget is *to manage your expectations*. Even if the task sounds simple to you, remember, you are dealing with a toddler. Learn to manage your expectations based on his abilities. For instance, he can help put his dirty clothes away in the laundry basket, but you cannot expect him to load the washing machine or fold his clothes. You can engage him while you do these things so he learns from your actions. Don't forget to appreciate his efforts; after all, he is trying his best.

Creating a Routine

Adults don't need a routine chart, but it would probably help us if we had one. When you have a specific routine, you know what's to be done at a point. Don't wonder, "What do I do now?" It equals putting your daily routine on autopilot. When you create a routine chart for your little one, it helps in the same way. After all, he is still learning, and to make things easier, use the chart.

It is also a great way to teach him how to manage his time and life in general. When you have a specific routine for your toddler, it allows him to experience different activities without excessive stimulation. If you constantly tell your toddler what he needs to do or should do, it can become frustrating for both of you. Instead, put all the tasks he needs to do in a chart form.

A common mistake many parents make is they forget that their primary responsibility towards their toddler is to make themselves obsolete. It might not sound pleasant, but you need to ensure that your child can take care of himself. When you give him certain responsibilities at home, it makes him feel independent. When he completes such activities, he will feel more confident. These feelings will stay with him throughout his life. However, it doesn't mean a routine chart is a silver bullet. Sometimes, he makes a mistake, and there will be resistance and lots of challenges along the way. However, it does provide a streamlined way of dealing with all these things without giving up.

The simplest way to avoid struggles in the morning or during bedtime is using this tool. Sit with your toddler and ask him all the things he needs to do before going to sleep. For instance, if his bedtime ritual includes a warm bath, changing into nightclothes, story time with his parents, singing a lullaby, and so on, <u>make a note</u>. Ask him what else he would like to add to all this. If he has any changes to make, consider his suggestions, and use them as helpful insights.

By allowing your toddler to be a part of this process, and creating his routine chart, he will feel more confident and capable. Instead of telling him what he needs to do next, you can point to this chart and ask him what he should be doing. For instance, before going to bed at night, a simple activity, you can ask him what clothes he wants to wear the following day. Once he chooses these clothes, it reduces the hassle of getting dressed in the morning. This comes in handy, especially if he goes to daycare or will be attending preschool.

Here is a simple example of a routine chart
- 7:30 AM-wake-up
- 8:00 AM- Potty and brushing
- 9:00 AM- Breakfast

In summary:
- Start creating a routine chart with your little one.
- Ask him what he would want to do and include these tasks in the charts.
- Whenever your little one accomplishes a task, take a picture of him doing it and place it next to the activity.
- Don't deviate from the routine charts, stick to them as much as you can.
- Don't add any unnecessary awards; focus only on completing the task.

There are no breaks when it comes to parenting, and parenting a toddler is a full-time responsibility. Use the hints provided to help you both and avoid any unpleasantness at home.

Chapter Ten: Growing Out Of Toddlerdom

Children grow up quickly. It might feel like it was only yesterday when you laid your eyes on your baby for the first time, and now, he is close to starting preschool. It can make one wonder where all the time went. Watching your child grow and develop is exciting and thrilling. However, change is seldom easy, but it can be handled effectively with a little planning and preparation.

Growing out of toddlerdom brings with it a variety of changes. The best thing you can do as your child's primary caregiver is to anticipate these changes and prepare yourself for it. Preparation helps eliminate uncertainty and anxiety associated with major life milestones, such as starting preschool. In this chapter, you will learn about the different tips you can follow to help you and your toddler prepare yourselves for the end of toddlerdom.

Preparing Your Toddler

Your toddler is learning and growing; change is an important part of this process. Don't just spring the idea of going to preschool on your toddler at the last instance. Instead, slowly prepare him for it. If you ensure that he is excited about this change, it becomes easier and more positive. Here are simple ideas you can use to increase his excitement and mentally condition him for the end of a toddler world.

If you and your toddler enjoy bedtime stories, include preschool stories. These days, there are different books available about preschool and choose one that appeals to you. You can sit together, read through the stories, or even choose an interactive storybook. Explain the story to him and ask how he feels about the character going to preschool. Ensure that you always maintain a positive attitude about it.

As mentioned in the previous chapter, toddlers are creative and imaginative. A simple way to get accustomed to going to preschool, while capitalizing on his creativity and imagination, is by playing pretend. You can use pretend play and encourage him to explore going to preschool. You can take turns pretending to be the child, parent, and teacher. From acting out a daily routine, such as waking up in the morning, having breakfast, going to preschool, and waving goodbye to reading stories, circle time, taking naps, and playing outside, there are different activities you can work on. It helps reassure your toddler that preschool does not differ that much from staying at home. The only difference is he gets to meet other kids. You can also warm him up to the idea of growing up by saying "big kids attend preschool." If he has any questions or worries about it, ensure that you carefully and patiently address all his concerns. You will learn more about this in the next sections.

Ensure that you take your child to his preschool and explore its surroundings before it starts. A tour of the preschool, playground, and different activities they conduct will prepare him for the actual upcoming events.

There are different small skills your toddler needs to perfect before going to preschool. Don't be worried if he doesn't get the hang of it yet, but he will once he goes there. Children are curious and learn better when they see others their age do the same things. A simple way to increase his self-help skills is by making a game of it. The simple skills you can teach him are putting on his backpack, unzipping his coat, trying on his shoes, and so on. For instance, create a competitive race. Use a stopwatch to check how long he takes to put on his shoes. If he needs to carry lunch or snacks to the preschool, get him used to eating from a lunch box. You can have a few "picnics" and pretend he is at preschool. This gives him a chance to open his lunchbox, unwrap his snacks, and so on.

If he is worried about missing his parents, sibling, or pets, you can give him a family photograph to take to preschool. He can also talk about his family with his peers and teachers.

Preparing Yourself

You have reached a major milestone if your child is starting preschool soon. There will be a variety of conflicting emotions running while through your mind. You will be excited about the fun your child will have, and the new journey he is setting out on. Simultaneously, it is also natural for parents to feel a little sad and anxious that their child is growing up. He was a tiny tot just a few months ago! All these emotions are common, and all parents experience them. However, with some preparation, the transition becomes easier.

Preparing your toddler for preschool is as important as preparing yourself. Yes, even parents need to prepare themselves emotionally and mentally for the moment of separation. Until now, you were probably used to spending all your time with your toddler. Now that he is nearing preschool, you need to get used to spending some time away from them. Perhaps the most difficult part of this is the first goodbye. Ensure that you maintain a positive and upbeat tone. If your child notices your apprehension, he will feel scared, too. Therefore, think of a special goodbye routine wherein you could kiss him on his palm and tell him to hold onto it all day long, or a special hug before he leaves. Ensure you resist the urge to go back into the preschool and rescue your toddler. This is an important step for him, and it is quintessential in his journey to adulthood. The first step matters a lot, and therefore, ensure that you are loving, kind, supportive, and compassionate to him.

To help with first-goodbye jitters and separation anxiety on his first day of the preschool, wait for a while after waving goodbye (about 15-20 minutes) to ensure that the transition becomes easy for your little one. You could also explore the classroom environment with your toddler to ensure that he is comfortable. *Usually, the parents struggle more than the toddler in accepting the change.*

Dealing with Worries

Starting preschool is a major change for your toddler, and he might have questions, concerns, or even worries about it. All these things are natural, and you should encourage open and honest discussions about it. There are two simple steps to address his worries and concerns. The first step is to listen to whatever your child has to say, and the second step is to notice any non-verbal messages he might be communicating

Being A Good Listener

Your child might not be able to articulate what he is feeling fully. However, that does not mean he has no worries. Whenever he starts talking to you about it, don't brush away his worries or write them off as silly. At the same time, don't jump into quickly and reassure him without even listening to what he has to say. It can be tempting to reassure him and soothe his worries but listening to him is also important. No matter how big or small his worries are, they are his concerns, and if you don't listen, it merely invalidates his feelings. If an adult listens to his concerns, especially one of his primary caregivers, it helps improve his self-esteem and confidence. Imagine how you would feel if someone wrote off your worries as silly.

When your child is talking about his worries is to be patient. If he has any worries or concerns when he starts preschool, it can influence his overall experience. To ensure he has the best possible experience, his mind should be free from worries. There could be some simple questions such as "Will my teacher be nice?" "Will I be able to make friends?" "What if I don't like it?" or "What if you forget to pick me up?" These worries might sound silly to an adult but are quite scary for your little one. Therefore, be a patient and compassionate listener.

Talk to him about the different feelings he might be experiencing. Tell him it is okay to feel happy, scared, excited, or even worried. Once you talk to him about these feelings, it will help ease his worries. Even adults feel better when we are told our worries are common, don't we? Talk to your child and tell him it is okay to feel a variety of emotions whenever we start something new. You can give examples from your life to make him more comfortable. Children often think adults don't experience feelings and emotions as they do. There might have been times when, as a child, you thought your parents, "Just don't get it." Well, times have changed, and the roles have reversed. You could share your own experiences. Even saying, "Honey, it is okay to be scared. Even mommy gets scared when she must do something new," can be helpful. If you have these conversations while following the tips mentioned in the previous sections, it will help make him feel more comfortable about going to preschool.

Being A Good Observer

Toddlers are talkative. Despite how much he talks, most 3-year-olds aren't good at explaining what they might be feeling or their worries. Therefore, watch his behavior. Kids act out whenever there's a major change involved and going to preschool is one such change. Different ways of acting out include withdrawing himself from his usual activities, excessive clinging, or aggressiveness. When children face a major lifestyle change, there can be a regression in certain areas. For instance, your little one might be potty trained, but if you notice he is having accidents, it is a sign of regression. It essentially means he is not coping well with a major change, and it is causing drastic changes in other established behaviors. If you notice he is constantly asking you to feed or clothe him, it's also a sign he isn't coping well. Parents can feel a little frustrated when they noticed their toddlers and aggressive behavior. You might also believe that if you keep helping him, he wouldn't do these things on his own or forget the desirable behaviors.

The best course of action is to simply let him go through this phase, and it will end. During this period, all that he needs is your support, unconditional love, encouragement, and lots of patience.

The concepts of positive discipline and parenting don't end once your toddler starts preschool. The basic techniques and tips discussed in this book can be used for parenting kids of all age groups. The only thing you need to change is the way you apply them. For instance, offering choices, information, communication of emotions, and understanding the kid's perspectives can be used whether you are parenting a toddler or a teenager. So, never stop using positive discipline, and you will be pleasantly surprised as you see your little one grow into a confident, self-assured, and independent adult with wonderful manners.

Conclusion

Now that you've gone through the different suggestions, tips, techniques, and strategies in this book, your idea of parenting will change. Learning about positive parenting and implementing positive discipline principles will help raise a child who is happy, confident, and well-adjusted to life. It also helps strengthen the bond you share with your little one. Your child might be the apple of your eyes, but sometimes, things get difficult. Parenthood isn't always about fun and games. You need to alternate between the roles of playing a good and a bad cop.

For children, their parents are not only their guardians and caretakers, but also their friends, mentors, and role models. Most things that kids learn are often from their parents. Therefore, playing the role of a parent is important and crucial in your child's development. By setting a good example, you are encouraging your toddler to follow. Dealing with a child doesn't mean you have to raise your voice or dole out punishments. Instead, it's about communicating with your child and avoid certain behaviors by making him realize the difference between good and bad behaviors.

Discipline is one area a lot of parents struggle with. If you face any guilt in this aspect, cut yourself some slack. Loving your child means disciplining him, too. Discipline is the simplest way to ensure he does nothing that puts him in harm's way. From learning about dealing with tantrums to fixing any misbehavior and building self-esteem and confidence, positive discipline comes in handy.

In this book, you were introduced to simple tips and techniques you can follow to successfully potty train your toddler. If bedtime seems like an uphill battle, and every night makes you feel drained out and tired, try either of the sleep training tactics discussed in this book. Besides this, there is one simple rule you must always remember- positive parenting starts at you and with you. The sooner you start, the better it is to use these tactics for parenting your little one.

Now that you are armed with all the information you need, the next step is to implement the simple strategies, suggestions, and tips in this book. Remember, parenting is an ongoing process. It takes a lot of patience, consistency, effort, dedication, and unconditional love. Once all these elements are in place, sprinkle them with positive discipline and voila- you can raise your toddler to be a happy, well-adjusted, and confident child.

Part 2: Potty Training

An Essential Step-By-Step Guide to Having Your Toddler Go Diaper Free Fast, Including Special Methods for Boys and Girls

Introduction

Do you want to potty-train your child but don't know where to start? Well, say goodbye to all your worries. In this book, we shall discuss every single facet of potty-training in a very thorough manner. We will be covering every single base that concerns the training process, from picking the right time to potty-train your toddler to ditching diapers in a hassle-free way.

The book explores ten topics that revolve around potty-training that will make the entire process easier on your nerves, manageable to your schedule, and easy for your child.

When is the right time to potty-train? Is there such a thing as potty-training your child too early? Too late? What are signs that they are ready for potty-training? How should you start their training?

Then, we'll bust myths that surround potty-training, such as early potty-training can cause bladder damage. Spoiler alert, there's no truth to it. We'll discuss a total of sixteen of these myths before moving on to how you can get your toddler to bid adieu to diapers.

We'll further delve into the psychology of potty-training and how a botched training can result in lasting psychological damage to your child.

How should you make your child use the potty for the first time? Which is the better option for them, the potty, or the toilet seat?

We'll also expound on the problems that may arise in the potty-training process.

Did you know that there's a marked difference between daytime potty-training and nighttime potty-training? The biggest difference is the child's development. We'll elucidate how to go about nighttime potty-training and the precautions to take.

Is potty-training a boy different from a girl? Yes. The eighth chapter covers those differences.

What is a surefire way to build your child's potty habit? We shall talk about methods that embed this habit in their little minds, making them stick to a routine throughout the day, and eventually, throughout their lives.

Last, this book involves the transition from potty to an adult toilet and what the transition entails.

If those points and questions mentioned above have occurred to you throughout your child's training, buy this book and read it cover to cover! It contains thoroughly researched, fact-checked, concise information that shall make you a potty-training expert in a matter of a few hours.

From step-by-step instructions to succinct bullet points, this book is written in a casual, friendly, and easy-to-comprehend way that helps you understand the training process deeply and clearly. We have left no stone unturned in this guide to getting your toddler diaper-free.

Potty-training a child is no easy feat. It's one of the biggest challenges a parent can face in their child's development. We have meticulously rooted out every single aspect of the training and explained it in an intuitive manner that will be beneficial for you and your toddler.

Chapter One: When to Start Potty-Training

Potty-training is an important milestone for you and your child, with its success depending on several factors such as the physical, mental, behavioral, and developmental changes in your child's life rather than just their age. However, most children display signs they are ready for potty-training somewhere between the ages of 18 months to 24 months. This is not a hard and fast rule, though, as some children might not display those signs before they are at least 3 years of age.

To ascertain if your child is ready for potty-training or not, ask yourself these questions:

- Is my child able to walk to the toilet and sit on it?
- Is my child able to pull their pants up and down?
- Does my child stay dry for longer spells, such as two hours?
- Is my child able to comprehend and follow my instructions? (Basic instructions; not advanced tasks)
- Does my child convey the need to go to the toilet verbally and non-verbally?

- Does my child appear to be interested in going to the toilet?

If most answers to those questions were yes, your child is probably ready to start potty-training. If most answers to those questions was no, then it might be better to wait.

Although it is agreed that the best time to start potty training is when your child shows signs of readiness, but another readiness must be accounted for: yours. Instead of appearing too eager for the training to your child, let them, with their own motivation, take the lead. Another thing to remember here is that your child's success or difficulty in the potty-training does not connote to their intelligence. And since this is a training process, they will inevitably make mistakes and make accidents throughout. This does not call for punishment. There is no room for punishment in the potty-training process.

Here, I summarize the series of steps you can follow to make sure things go smoothly after you have determined that your child and you are ready to begin potty-training:

1. Pick Out Positive Reinforcement Phrases

Choose a selection of words to say to your toddler when referring to their potty-training. Positive reinforcement goes a long way in making them feel encouraged and involved in the process. When referring to their bodily fluids, such as their urine and their poop, avoid using negative phrases such as "made a stinky" or "dirtied your pants." This will make them associate the activity as something shameful or reprehensible, which will put them off from their training.

2. Make Sure All the Equipment is Prepped in Advance

We're talking about potty chairs and stools in the bathroom so that when they visit the toilet, they can easily prop themselves up on the stool and sit on the potty chair. Have them take a dry run (with their clothes still on) on the chair to acquaint them with it. Ask them how it feels. Have them put their feet on the stool to make them comfortable while sitting on the chair. Again, use positive phrases for the toilet. You can show them the purpose of the toilet by emptying a dirty diaper in it and asking them to flush it.

3. Keep a Schedule

Schedule regular potty breaks, such as in the morning right after they wake up and after every nap they take. In addition, schedule a break every two hours and make them sit on the toilet (or potty chair) with no diaper. With boys, have them practice peeing sitting down on the toilet first. Then, once they have mastered that, show them how to do it while standing up. During your child's scheduled potty breaks, accompany them and either talk to them or interact with them by playing with a toy or reading them their favorite story.

4. Respond Quickly

Take your child to the toilet immediately when you see the signs such as squatting, grunting, squirming, wincing, and grabbing their genital area. Your quick response will help them associate their discomfort with the need to go to the toilet. Praise them throughout, such as telling them they did well to tell you they had to go to the toilet. While potty-training your child, you should keep them in comfortable, loose clothes, so there's less hassle for both them and you in terms of removing them.

5. Teaching Them the Hygienic Way

Explain basic hygiene to your child, such as wiping with toilet paper once they are done. For girls, you must teach to wipe front to back (up to down) so they prevent any germs and fecal particles from making their way to their bladder or vagina. Instruct your child they must always wash their hands afterward. Once you have covered the basics, tell them they have to flush the toilet and put the lid down.

6. Bid Adieu to the Diapers

Once you and your child have progressed past the first few weeks of this critical process, it's time to ditch the diapers in favor of underwear or training pants. This is a big step for both of you, and it's recommended that you celebrate it with them. However, if you feel they cannot stay dry, you can revert them to diapers. There's no rushing this final leg of the process.

What if they are not getting the hang of it?

If you feel like your child is having difficulty in staying dry or that they cannot stick to the schedule, maybe they are not ready for potty-training yet. You can try again in a few months. If, however, you notice they aren't ready and, despite that, try to force them to acclimatize, it may backfire on you. You don't want to create a power struggle or make them rebel. Both of you are on the same team here.

What do I do when accidents happen?

Accidents will happen. When they do, do not scold your child, do not discipline them by way of punishment, and, most important, do not guilt-trip or shame them. Staying calm and remaining positive will go a long way in making sure that they don't repeat the mistake.

Keep diapers, a change of clothes, and extra underwear on hand, so that when or if an accident happens, you can quickly change their clothes, especially in a daycare or school setting.

Toddler Development and Potty-Training

Before establishing the appropriate time for starting potty-training, let us look at the development stages of a child. According to the Nemours Foundation, there are six stages of your child's development. They are:

1 Year (12 Months)

Your baby is a toddler now. They will walk soon if they haven't already. They will explore previously unexplored areas, becoming freer in their locomotion and interaction with the environment.

In terms of communication, they will point to things and vocalizing their recognition, they will wave hello and goodbye, they will babble so it mimics talking. Most important, they will call you and your partner by "mama" and "papa."

About movement, your toddler will stand on their own, walking with either one hand held or alone, play with toy cubes and shapes and bang them together, be able to grip things with their full hand and use their hands to pick up chunks of food to bring to their face during mealtimes.

They will enjoy games like peekaboo. They will enjoy story time, being read to, and looking at bright, vivid pictures in picture books. They will express displeasure when you leave the room by way of crying. They will feel happy and become gleeful when they accomplish something new, such as walking a relatively longer distance, creating a tower of blocks, or succeeding in a simple game.

Cognitively, they can follow simple commands, imitate their elder siblings and parents, and be able to turn the pages of a book to picture that they like better than the others. They will also vie for your attention by doing something like dropping their toy, wailing, or laughing.

15 Months

At this age, your toddler will become more expressive about their wants and needs. However, their increasing capacity for the verbal enunciation of what they want (such as their pointing to an object and making a sound) means they will also throw tantrums when they don't get their way. While dealing with their tantrums, realize that they are an essential and very normal part of your child's development. You can distract them from their tantrums by indulging them in a game. And at the very least, you, being the adult, can keep calm when they're throwing a tantrum.

Communicatively, they will indicate their want by pointing at something, pulling at it, or grunting loudly. They will bring you their favorite book to be read or their favorite toy to play with. They will, besides saying "mama" and "papa," pick up a few new words and use them properly. If you playfully ask them, "where are your ears?" they can point to their body parts.

They will take more steps without your support. They can squat if they want to pick up something. they will be able to drink from a cup or a glass. They can stack toy cubes and doodle on paper with coloring pencils and crayons.

They will exhibit preferences for certain activities over others. They will use blankets, comforters, and teddy bears or other stuffed animals for self-comfort. They'll be better able to show their affection for you or a caregiver by kissing and hugging. Their dislikes, for things such as loud noises, will become more expressive.

Your child will understand simple commands and may follow them, depending on the mood they're in. They'll start mimicking what you do around the house, such as reading a book or watching TV. Around this time, it would be best to introduce them to problem-solving games, such as jigsaw puzzles.

1.5 Years (18 Months)

Around the time they're 1-1/2 years old, your toddler's growth will have slowed down a bit as compared to their first year of development. That is because babies grow at a faster rate than toddlers. Even though it will appear that their physical growth has somewhat decelerated, your child is still learning so much every day in terms of language, coordination, and balance.

An 18-month-old toddler can pronounce 10 to 20 words clearly. They will understand and respond to simple, one-step commands such as "Please pick your toy up." They will recognize and point to their body parts when asked.

They'll be able to run, climb the stairs with some assistance, take their clothes off, throw a ball, and scribble with their coloring pencils and crayons.

They'll start engaging in pretend play and will laugh when others laugh. They will be better able to show affection and will form the coordination skills required to play with other children. And they will show their irritation through tantrums.

At this age, they can name their toys, or at least their favorite ones, name and point at familiar imagery in their favorite picture book. They can imitate you by mimicking you sweeping the floor, cooking in the kitchen or talking to someone on the phone. They'll be able to match a pair of similar objects.

2 Years (24 Months)

This is the ideal time when potty-training comes into play. You can pick up on your child's cues, such as their interest in going to the toilet on their own, displaying signs they know the need to go to the toilet, and expressing their need to you.

In terms of communication, your child can now say 50 words or more. They'll be able to form basic sentences, sentences that even a stranger can comprehend. They'll use real words instead of made-up baby words, like calling "breakfast" breakfast instead of, say, "num-num."

They'll be able to run better, play with a ball by kicking or throwing it, walk up and down stairs without assistance (but please make sure to supervise them as they do so), be able to basic shapes, and sometimes they'll be able to feed themselves when food is put in front of them.

While previously they'd been able to follow one-step commands, now they'll be able to follow two-step commands, such as "Please pick your toy up and bring it to me." They'll grow more aware of their body and will be able to name more of their body parts. They'll engage in play-time with their toys more interactively, like feeding their teddy bear or doll or mimicking taking care of it like it was their baby.

2.5 Years (30 Months)

The most pronounced growth of your toddler at this age is in their vocabulary. They can now say more than a few hundred words. You can cultivate their sense of vocabulary by teaching them nursery rhymes, playing songs, and reading books to them.

They can speak phrases that comprise of three to four words. Other people can understand them more than half the time. They'll start using pronouns and they'll ask questions along the "what?" and "where?" lines.

They'll be able to wash their hands, dry their hands, brush their teeth with some assistance, pull their pants up, jump when they're joyful, and throw a ball with their hand.

In terms of social and emotional development, they'll participate in pretend play and enjoy it. They will participate in playing with other kids more proactively. They can tell you when they need to go to the toilet or when they need a diaper change. They'll be able to refer to themselves by their name.

Cognitively, they'll develop their sense of humor. Silly stories and funny baby jokes will appeal to them and make them laugh. They will understand the concept of things and items.

3 Years

When they are three years old, your toddler's imagination will soar. As a result, they'll start taking part in more make-believe games. But sometimes, their imagination will get the better of them and scare them. Benign shadows may appear as evil entities and spook them out. During this phase, listen to your child and reassure them.

In terms of language skills, they'll be able to form sentences with three or more words. You'll be able to understand what they're saying most of the time. This is an inquisitive age, at which they'll ask, "why?" a lot.

They'll be able to walk up and down the stairs with their feet alternating. When playing with a ball, they'll be able to catch it with both their hands. They'll try to balance on one foot and succeed sometimes. They'll be able to dress and undress with your assistance.

At this age, they will be potty-trained for the daytime. If they have a friend, they'll be able to refer to them by name. They'll also start identifying gender and begin referring to people as "him" or "her." They will also start to develop a sense of turn-based games, where they'll wait for their turn.

So, when should you start potty-training?

The best time to start training your child is when they begin showing signs that they are ready.

Children are unable to start using the toilet until they are somewhere between 18 months and three years. Girls are quicker to adapt to this than boys. Most parents will start training their children somewhere between two to three years.

Some parents follow a method called elimination communication, where they potty-train their child as young as four months. They will take their child immediately to the toilet when they see signs that they're about to pee or poop. Professionals do not recommend this method. It has been shown to cause complications later in life, such as difficulties when using the toilet in a public place like school.

It's also crucial to note that toddlers cannot control their bladder and their rectal muscles until they're at least 18 months year old. Therefore, it is important to wait for signs that they are ready to start potty-training.

Signs That Your Toddler is Ready for Potty-Training

Previously, we discussed some developmental milestones at various ages of your toddler. Those skills are somewhat of a prerequisite to their potty-training. As with other skills such as sitting up, crawling, walking, potty-training is an acquired skill and is best taught when your child's development (emotional and physical) is passed a certain point.

The key for potty-training is your child's desire for control, independence, self-mastery, and approval, i.e., their emotional readiness. Starting their potty-training before your child is ready can cause frustration on both ends.

Here are signs that you should look out for to gauge if your child is ready or not:

1. They begin Displaying Interest

When your child takes a keen interest in staying dry, staying clean, that's when you start potty-training them. Other signs of their interest to look out for are their piqued curiosity when you go to the toilet and their interest in wearing "big kid" underwear as opposed to diapers.

2. They Stay Dry for Longer Spells

If your child can stay dry for at least two hours, it's a sign that their bladder capacity has increased, which shows they are ready for potty-training.

3. They Know When They Go

After your child has done a number one or two in their diaper, they'll start showing signs like hiding behind the curtains or the furniture. They'll probably go to another room to poop or pee. That's another sign that signifies that they are recognizing when they are going. Training your child before this time will likely cause complications, as your child will not be aware of when they are going, and since they won't know it, they won't be able to understand it.

4. They Exhibit Independence

Look out for phrases such as "I can do it myself, mommy!" These cues signify a desire to become more independent, which is an important milestone for potty-training. However, if they're not ready, such as when they're going through stress (adapting to a newborn) or change (moving to a new house), it's better to delay the training till both you and the child are back to being comfortable.

5. They Can Take Their Clothes Off

Your child should be able to pull their pants up and down. While they didn't have a reason to do this in the past, now they do. It's an acquired skill, one of many during the potty-training process, and you should make it easier by dressing your child in loose, easy-to-take-off clothing. Avoid clothes like rompers, tights, pants with zippers or belts, and any tight clothes that they'll have difficulty taking off.

6. They Can Follow Your Directions

Going to the toilet poses as challenges for your child, these challenges being: finding the toilet, turning on the bathroom's light, pulling down their pants, using a stool to get on the potty/toilet, relieving themselves, using toilet paper to wipe themselves, flushing, and last, washing their hands. If they're able to follow your directions with potty-training, they are ready to begin.

7. They Can Sit Still

Potty-training requires patience on the child's part. If they can sit still for extended periods without getting irritated, they can do so on the potty too.

8. They Can Walk and Run

If your child cannot walk or run properly, they aren't yet ready to start potty-training, as a major component of the training relies on them rushing quickly to the toilet whenever they feel like they have to go.

Chapter Two: Potty-Training Myths and Misconceptions

The territory of potty-training is riddled with myths and misconceptions. These are propagated by everyone from Cathy next door to some shady newsletter you keep getting in your email; all because of that one time you accidentally fed your address to some website offering you 20% off all baby clothing from their store. Separating fact from fiction is critical here because believing the myths and carrying them out will do you and your child more harm than good. Remember what Gandhi said, "Don't believe everything you read on the internet." Let's discuss some common myths and disprove them while we are at it.

1. Potty-Training too early will cause Complications like Constipation

You might have heard this one before from "veteran" parents now on their third or fourth child. Facebook mom groups and other social media platforms perpetuate that early training will cause your child to withhold, refuse to the toilet, and damage them psychologically. This is simply not true.

It does not depend on when you start the training as much as it depends on how you train them. If your approach to their training is gentle and makes sure that it keeps with the child's pace, no problems will occur. Scientifically, there is no connection between early potty-training and these issues. But there's research that states that early potty-training helps reduce the risk of toileting refusal, stool holding, and constipation.

Another research highlights the benefits of early potty-training, stating that infants can be potty trained by as early as 12 months if the training is done gentle and keeps the child's natural instincts in consideration. The child can go to the toilet independently by the time they're 24 months old.

Some things harmful to your child include punishing them, forcing them to push, and running the tap to hasten them. By including potty time in your child's routine early on, you can eliminate these aforementioned issues.

2. The Child has to be Ready before You Can Start Potty-Training

According to a study conducted by Douglas and Bloomfield in 1988, before the disposable diapers were invented—this is around the '70s—parents put their babies on potties right after they learned how to sit up, the babies, not the parents. Almost half of the babies, around the time they turned 12 months old, had stopped using diapers, and almost 80% were completely potty-trained by the time they were 18 months old. Other statistic-based research suggests that babies and toddlers are ready for and very much capable of potty-training when they reach 18 months and that the best time for ditching diapers is around 18 months to 30 months.

A pediatrician named Terry Brazelton developed the theory of "readiness" in the 1960s. Terry proposed this idea that children have to be ready before they're able to start potty-training. However, this theory, although it had some good ideas as its basis, was not sound, as most of the literature that Terry wrote was jarring and contradictory and missed major points about the child's development's in relation to potty-training commencement. Furthermore, Terry Brazelton was paid by Pampers to endorse their diapers. Many researchers say this made Brazelton turn his research into a marketing ploy to sell more disposable nappies, encouraging parents to let their children stay in diapers for longer to sell more Pampers rather than train their children.

The age that defines readiness for a child depends upon the skills they learn. These skills may be taught either socially or culturally. They need to have essential skills pre-developed, such as motor skills, to get trained. However, some parents do not consider these pre-requisites and instead instruct their toddlers earlier than the recommended time.

3. The Bladder Gets Damaged Due to Early Potty-Training

As with other myths, this is false. Regularly going to the toilet protects your child's urinary bladder rather than damage it. By making them go to the toilet regularly, you help develop your child's sphincter control from a very early age. Training your child between the ages of 15 months to 24 months reduces the risk of bladder damage and bladder infection. It also reduces the risk of their wetting the bed. It improves their bladder function.

The urinary bladder is a muscle, and like other muscles, using it regularly strengthens it. Using it consciously, such as in potty-training, strengthens it further and ensures the establishment of a messaging system between their bladder and their brain. This system ensures the development of control and awareness in your child. There's research-based evidence that infants have bladder control from their birth and that they can learn to coordinate their urination as early as 9 months.

All toileting problems arise from your child's holding their poop or their pee. These problems include accidents involving poop, urinary frequency, bed-wetting, and urinary tract infections. Early potty-training helps reduce the risk of these accidents, ensures good bladder coordination, reduces the chances of their contracting infections, protects the bladder, and promotes staying dry during the daytime.

4. It's the Child that Decides When Potty-Training Happens, Not the Parent

This is one of those myths that sound like they have an element of truth to them but are false, overall. Yes, it's better that you let the child be a bit eager before starting their potty-training, but that does not mean that the entire decision is in their hands. They're just a child. You're the parent. Brazelton's research proposed that the child must be ready before you start their training, but later, more recent research conducted by Berk in 1990 stated that the whole process of potty-training gets wrapped up faster when the parent takes the reins of the process. This means you devote specific portions of time in the day to make sure that your child puts in consistent effort in their training. Remember, their readiness is not an innate trait that will just manifest itself one day out of nowhere. Their readiness depends upon the parent introducing the concept of potty-training to them and easing them into it. Your child will be interested in potty-training only if you help instill that interest in them. They can go to the toilet on their own only if you teach them the required skills.

If, however, you do follow that myth and let the child decide when they're ready, it will cause complications later on in their life. For example, introducing potty-training after your child is 24 months old will increase the risk of delayed bladder control and daytime wetting. Furthermore, if you delay it beyond the age of three years, it will create environmental, economic, and social complications.

5. Pull-Up Pants are Useful for Potty-Training

The entire marketing strategy behind pull-ups is that they're beneficial for potty-training. Here's how that's not exactly true. Pull-ups are a short-term comfort, both for the child and the parent. You as a parent, will be appealed by pull-ups avoiding potty-training accidents, such as leaking, bed-wetting, and so on. And you would be right to believe that. But here's the thing, pull-ups absorb the wetness, staying dry even after your child has urinated in them. In that regard, they work exactly like diapers. A research conducted by Rogers in 2002, states that because of that reason, pull-ups do not help in the potty-training process.

Another research study states that using pull-ups was less effective when trying to cultivate urinary consistency in a child.

While a child is a potty-training, they are essentially ditching an old way (the diapers) in favor of a new one. When you use pull-ups, you confuse the child by making them stick to the old way while also trying to teach them a new one. So, for the sake of the training, you shouldn't use pull-ups while potty-training your child.

6. Children Can Only Stay Dry Once their Hormones Have Developed

Okay. This one's a bit tricky, as hormones do play a factor in suppressing urine production. These hormones work for most children, but this doesn't mean that the myth is true. If your toddler or baby can stay dry during the day, thanks to your potty-training, they're likely to stay dry at night, despite whether their hormones have developed or not. This might surprise you, but if you've trained your baby from as early as six months, they'll be able to stay dry at night as they're no longer accustomed to the diaper.

7. Potty-Training Gets Done Quicker if You Start it Later

False! It takes the same time to potty-train a child early as it does later. Earlier, it's not recommended that you teach them potty-training after three years of age, because it will cause complications such as the increased risk for bed-wetting and soiling. The ideal time to start potty-training your child is between 18 to 24 months. Even if you take longer, such as after 25 months, it will take the same time. There's no rushing the process. There's no shortcut that will allow you to do it quicker. It's going to take time either way. Earlier potty-training is related to your child's acquiring urinary confidence, and not because of bladder dysfunction. If your child uses the potty early, they will develop that confidence and will ask you to take them to the potty sooner.

8. It's Easier to Train Girls Than Boys

Here's another classic myth that is not grounded in truth, whatsoever. It takes the same time to train a boy as it does for a girl. It's not a gender-based skill. Whether you're training a boy or a girl, the potty-training process should remain the same. Most parents, under the impression that boys are harder to train than girls, complicate the process needlessly for their child. Don't do that. They're both equally able to learn potty-training at the same pace.

9. Placing the Child on the Potty Forcibly Will Train Them

Not even a little bit. It might backfire. It might cause them to throw tantrums and develop irritability. But one thing it won't do: train them. There's a ton of parents who still hold to this myth as fact. This is a major misconception that needs to be rooted out right away. Remember, if you force your child, you're going to cause them to fear the potty. You're going to make them reel at the sight of it. If you keep on doing that, it will become a power struggle that will end up in a fight, and we know how these fights play out. The parent has to give up at the end because frankly, there's not much you can do when your child is wailing non-stop.

What you can do to make the transition easier is to communicate with your child and allow them to learn the signs they need to go. Communicate with them about it. Once they're aware of these signs (the signs we discussed in the previous chapter), they'll come to you themselves. As opposed to something that they fear, potty-training will become something that they'll look forward to.

10. Daycare Will Take Care of My Child's Potty-Training for Me

Uh-uh. No sir. Most daycares will turn you down if you haven't trained your child on your own, and the ones that do accept your child, they'll teach them potty-training in a way convenient for the daycare staff, i.e., a method involving pull-up pants and taking them to the potty every few hours. They will botch the potty-training process and cause numerous complications you will be left to deal with. It will boggle your child, resulting in the potty-training process taking longer than usual.

11. There's a Right Age for Potty-Training

Have you seen that meme with the pirate going, "Yes, but actually no?" It holds true for this myth. There's a right window for potty-training, sure, but there's no such thing as the right age for potty training. We've discussed that window. It is 18 to 24 months. But some parents are under the notion they should get their children off diapers by the time they're x months old. They forget that every child develops at their rate, and no two children are the same. While in some culture potty-training commences as early as nine months, and with some parents, they don't even train their child until they are three years of age. It all hinges on when your child has developed complementing traits that go along with potty-training.

12. You Should Celebrate and Applaud Your Child the First Time They Use the Potty

While it may seem like sound advice, another myth needs to be busted wide open. By appearing too enthusiastic, you might end up doing one of two things:

> a) You'll make your child think that they accomplished a great feat and that they should always be applauded whenever they go to the toilet

b) if your child is shy, it will make them avoid going to the toilet because they'll hate the confrontation and the celebratory nature of going to the toilet.

This does not mean you don't praise your child. You should, but without sounding too enthusiastic and eager. A simple "good job!" will suffice.

Similarly, using stickers and stickers and other methods of celebrating achievement will put too much pressure on the child to always perform so it warrants praise. They will become anxious with the pressure to perform.

13. Putting Underwear on Your Child Will Quicken the Process

It won't. It's going to make them feel feelings of failure when they'll eventually soil their underwear. It's going to make them feel shameful and confused. Only put underwear on your child once they're in the final leg of the potty-training process, not before.

14. It's Better to Have a Potty-Trained Child Than Have Them in Diapers

Enjoy the diapers while your child is still in them. Remember, once you've potty-trained your child, you must attend to them every time they need to go. This will be especially difficult when you're, say, traveling, and need to stop every time they have to go to the toilet. Keep diapers on hand for such occasions until your child can remain dry for longer periods. There's no rushing the process.

15. There's No Going Back Once You've Begun Potty-Training

It's not an irreversible process. Sometimes your child cannot grasp the fundamentals, and it will seem like they're not ready. Notice that cue. That's usually a sign you need to delay the training. Take a break of a few months and then start the training afresh. Your child is going through various developmental changes; changes will sometimes not coincide with their potty-training and make them uncomfortable and distressed.

16. Nighttime and Daytime Potty-Training Should be Taught at the Same Time

Nighttime potty-training is related to urine production, retention, and hormones. It's quite different from daytime potty-training. Daytime training is easier to pull off and thus should be taught many months before they're finally able for nighttime training. The two don't go together.

Hopefully, covering these myths will help you differentiate between fact and fiction, thus easing the process both for you and your child.

Chapter Three: Ditching Diapers (Without the Drama)

Is there a right age to ditch diapers?

As we have previously discussed, there isn't just one right age to start your child's potty-training. Similarly, there's no right age to stop using diapers, as both these things—i.e., the potty-training and the diaper ditching—go in tandem. Some kids might be early adopters, while others might be late bloomers. However, is there such a thing as the right age to stop using diapers?

There's a window, a pretty long window, comfortable for both early adopters and late bloomers. It is 18 months to 3 years. That's when most children are capable of starting potty-training. Remember, the first step is getting them to use the potty. The diaper ditching comes way after that, once your child is comfortable going to the toilet on their own and are not wetting the bed at night.

Starting the diaper ditching process too early will only result in frustration for both you and your child, as most babies and toddlers cannot control their bowel and bladder before the age of 18 months. If you attempt to get them to ditch their diapers before that age, it will be unsuccessful. It might make the child feel rebellious, reluctant, and nervous about the whole potty-training process.

Second, there's the whole element of keeping backup diapers at hand to consider. If your child sees that you've kept spare diapers around and you use them whenever they're unable to go to the toilet, they'll stop taking the training seriously and fall back on the diapers, which is something that we do not want. Once you're past the first trimester of the training process, remove the diapers as an option so your child knows that the only way they can relieve themselves is by going to the toilet.

Third, you might be wondering how long the potty-training process will take. Again, it depends on the child. It might take as little as a week, or it might take many months. The duration of the potty training depends on several factors, including the child's age, their interest, and their development. If they are on the younger side, it will take them longer. Longer as in some weeks. If they are showing interest on their own, take that as a cue they are eager to do the process faster. That means that it will take them just a couple of days. If they are hesitant or resistant, they will take more time.

Last, even though it depends on the individual, the approximate duration for potty-training is between 3 to 6 months. If that makes you feel overwhelmed, don't worry. You just have to take it day to day, and before you know it, your child will be trained, and those diapers will be redundant.

Choosing the Right Potty Goes a Long Way

The next major step in ditching diapers is choosing the right potty for your child. Why? Because choosing the potty can make or break the process. If you pick one that your child takes to, it will catalyze the whole training process faster. They'll like using that potty and will prefer it to their diapers.

When you go on a shopping trip to choose the potty, take your child with you and involve them in picking their favorite one. Two kinds of potties are available in the market these days: the seat reducer and the stand-alone potty. The seat reducer is cheaper and doesn't take up as much space as the stand-alone potty. The seat reducer goes on top of the regular toilet seat and reduces the size of the ring to make it comfortable for your kid. One major advantage of the reducer is that it accustoms your child to the regular toilet much faster than the stand-alone potty. To use a stand-alone potty, your child will have an easier time going to the toilet by themselves, and you can have the main toilet in the house all to yourself.

When selecting a stand-alone potty, take into account these three things: the simplicity of the potty, the fit, and safety. For example, if your child's butt barely fits on the rim, they will feel very uncomfortable while sitting on it, which will set back the whole process. Then, make sure that you get the right size, meaning your child's feet can touch the ground when they're sitting on it. If you can get a potty that has handles on it, it will help your child maintain their grip while they're relieving themselves, which will be a major advantage.

If you are getting a potty for a boy, one thing to consider is if the potty has a splash guard or not. The splash guard, although not necessary, will make it easier to clean the potty, minimizing the mess. The splash guard should be just about high to help keep the pee inside the potty but not too high it makes peeing a difficult challenge.

The potty you choose must be easy to clean and simple to use. If you are shopping online for a potty, read the reviews to see what your fellow parents are saying about it.

Let's Get Rid of the Diapers

When you have bought your potty or seat reducer, the next step is to get rid of the diapers gradually. Doing it right away is ill-advised as the child has yet to get used to their new mode of going. Do it once they have gone to the potty at least ten to twenty times. Once they are used to the potty, make the diapers disappeared. It's tempting to keep them as a fallback, but in the long term, it will only serve to deter the potty-training process, and we don't want that.

Disclaimer: the transition from diapers to potty will cause some accidents, so brace for that. This will be frustrating at the moment but will ultimately make your child stick to the potty and not rely on diapers.

Remember, when your child has learned that they can relieve themselves by going to the potty, their instinct will want them to stay clean. Every time they get dirty (whether by accident or in transition), they will feel extremely uncomfortable. That uncomfortableness will quicken their adaption to the potty, as they will learn that the potty is the hassle-free way to go to the toilet without dirtying themselves.

Some Do's and Don'ts

Here are some do's and don'ts to follow as you are transitioning your child from diapers to potty.

1. Observe the signs that your child needs to go. These signs include squirming, grunting, fiddling with something in their hands, shuffling their feet, making faces, trying to communicate whether by verbal or non-verbal cues they need to go. Whenever you see these signs, rush your child to the potty. That way, you'll be able to avoid any accidents and acquaint them with the potty organically.

2. Do not force your child into potty-training just because they have reached a certain age. If you have more than one kid, you'll

expect your toddler to learn at the pace your elder child learned. It's not the same for every child. While your elder child might have picked up on potty-training in a week or two, your toddler might not pick the habit that fast. Patience, as with other aspects of parenting, is key here.

3. We discussed dressing before, but it's so important that we will mention it again: dress your child in easy-to-take-off, loose clothes they can remove without a hassle whenever they need to go to the toilet. Overalls are a big no, with the exception that your child can very easily pull them off and put them back on without your help.

4. Do not listen to imposing relatives who pressurize you into getting your child out of diapers as early as you can. They are not there to deal with your child. Take their scolding advice and let it go from one ear and to the other one. If you feel overwhelmed by their advice, you will end up passing that tension to your child, making them feel stressed, which will set back the training.

5. Praise your child when they successfully go to the potty. But make sure not to go overboard with the praise, as it will make them associate praise with going to the potty, and they will start expecting it every time they use the potty. A simple pat or an encouraging phrase goes a long way in building their morale and confidence.

6. Do not engage in a battle of a power struggle with your child. Spoiler alert: They will always win. Why? Because while you have a rationale and logical thinking on your side, their trump card is irrationality and wailing and crying and throwing a tantrum. If they don't want to go, don't force them. Don't impose yourself on them needlessly. Pick your battles.

7. Let your child play with their favorite toy or read their favorite book to them while they are on the potty. If they get antsy when you're not there, keep them company as they go to the toilet.

8. Do not give nicknames to their body parts. Remember, we are trying to do the opposite of infantilizing them. Approaching the

training in a matter of fact and logical manner will cultivate the importance of the process in them.

9. Let your child have autonomy when going to the toilet. The more independent they will feel, the quicker they can adapt to potty-training, and the quicker they'll ditch their diapers.

10. Do not punish your child if they make a mess when not in diapers. This will reinforce in their minds that using the diapers was a good thing, as they never got punished while using them, and that not wearing the diapers is a bad thing, as they got punished.

11. Criticizing your child's potty going methods will also complicate things for both of you. It will make you frustrated and it will take their confidence away.

12. Patience is the name of the game, and as clichéd as it sounds, it's true. Potty-training, and subsequently diaper ditching, is a time-consuming process that will test your patience at times, but remember that this is the first time your child is going through such a radical change. Keep reminding them gently that their poop and pee needs to go in the potty and not on the floor or in their clothes. Your attitude is contagious and will ultimately decide how the training turns out. If you are there for them, patiently reassuring them along every step of the way, you will make them independent faster. Remember that as hard as it gets for you, it's not easy for your child either. They have only just gotten control of their bladder and bowels, and now they're being trained for something they don't have a clue about. Empathize with your child, reaffirm their struggle, and occasionally cheer them on my celebrating minor milestones.

Is there any wisdom to potty-training boot-camps?

Yes. That might seem a very hot take on boot-camps, but here's the reason they're insanely popular: they work in a very short time, which is the entire point of a boot-camp. You devote an entire week to give your child a crash course of sorts in potty-training, at the end of which you have ditched their diapers and have shifted them permanently to the potty. There are various boot-camps, such as the three-day boot-camp, the five-day boot-camp, and the one-week boot-camp, all with the same goal: getting your child off the diapers.

But note that as appealing as it sounds, it will be grueling for you during the entire duration, as you will be expected to ditch all your tasks and focus solely on the boot-camp.

Let's Briefly Cover What Standard Boot-Camp Demands

Pick a weekend on which you're free and have no upcoming plans. Notice the signs that your child is ready, then begin. On the first day, i.e., Saturday, get your child off the diapers and introduce training pants in the mix. We talked about the disadvantages of the training pants, but here's the thing: that was for regular potty-training and not boot-camps. The rules for boot-camps are different and thus allow a little leeway for using training pants. So, on Saturday, put on training pants on your child. These are reusable and can be washed again.

Then on the same day, introduce them to the potty and see if they're up for it. If they do not feel intimidated by it, they can ditch the training pants and use the potty.

Tell your child to listen to the signs of their body and learn which signs connote to their need to go to the toilet.

This weekend, you will take your child to the bathroom when they wake up, before every nap, after every nap, before and after every meal, and before they go to bed. Besides all these scheduled visits, just make sure that they go to the toilet every two hours.

It's going to be a very rigorous routine for the three days of the boot-camp, but at the end of it, you're going to have a child who has learned how to use the potty and ditch their diapers.

Keeping Some Cleaning Supplies on Hand

Once you have gone to the diaper ditching route, make sure that you have cleaning supplies on hand because you will need them.

Your child isn't expected never to make a mess. Between the transition from diapers to the potty, they will end up soiling their clothes or the house. But you'll be prepared for that. Stick up on the right cleaning supplies like Super-Sorbs for hard floors. They will soak up any pee, making it easier to clean. They can also absorb the smell, so you will have no rank smells coming from the floor after you're done cleaning. For other surfaces such as carpets or fabric, get something like Nature's Miracle or Rocco & Roxie. They're originally meant to be for pets, but many parents use them whenever some potty related accidents happen in the house. They can both remove stains and odors of pee and poop from the floors. Use nontoxic bleach for cleaning your child's underwear if they make a mess in them. For sanitizing surfaces, get disinfecting wipes that will clean up all the germs and fluids easily.

Some Techniques to Help Your Child Ditch their Diapers Without the Drama

Here are some parent-approved tips that will help your child transition to the potty with no fuss.

1. Turn the Training into a Game

There are ways to turn the potty-training routine into a game that your child actually looks forward to. Some parents put a Cheerio or a piece of Cheetos in the toilet and have their boy aim at it. This sparks their interest and makes them look forward to peeing in the toilet.

Some parents have tried putting food colors in the toilet so that whenever your child pees in it, the color changes, captivating their attention.

2. Turn Fear into Fun

Yes. Some children are afraid, and rightly so. Imagine it from their perspective. There's a big black hole in the toilet that they have to face every time they need to go. Some children might develop a phobia, while others will not think much of it. If your child shows signs they fear going to the toilet, it's time you swapped fear for fun by replacing their toilet with, say, a musical one. The musical toilet has a moisture activated sensor that plays nursery rhymes when the child pees or poops in it. If that doesn't help, keep them company and make their shift their focus from the toilet to you as you guide them and tell them not to be afraid.

3. Keep the Potty with You Wherever You Go

Whether you're sitting in the living room, the dining room, or the bedroom, take the potty with you wherever you and your child go. Have them sit at the potty at regular intervals, even if they have to go or not.

4. Encourage their Efforts

Praising them on their successes is well earned and all, but also encourage them whenever they make an effort. Some of those efforts will cause them falling, some will cause them making a mess, but it will eventually lead them to become potty-trained, so whenever they make an effort, say something reassuring.

5. Ditching the Pants at Home

When your child is at home, try ditching their pants and letting them roam naked around the house. This, although it appears to be strange, will help them adjust to the potty by helping them become more aware of their body and easily going to the potty without the hassle of clothing in their way.

6. Charts and Stars are a No-Go

Chalk that up to going overboard with the process. It might help initially in terms of encouragement and reassuring them, but it will make them accustomed to getting a new star on their chart every time they go, and be frank with yourself, sometimes you just don't have the energy to put in the enthusiasm. What will happen then?

Chapter Four: Potty-Pooping Psychology and Mental Preparedness

Mentally Preparing Your Child for Potty-Training

efore you can actively train your child, you must prepare them mentally. The first thing you can do, an easy task that requires little mental and physical effort, is teaching them by example. Children are receptive to what their parents do. You might have seen their mimicking behavior around the house. Mimicking is one of their primary modes of learning. With potty-training, the mimicking translates to them seeing you going to the toilet and becoming intrigued about what you're doing in there. If you're worried about the image of you going to the toilet being burned in their mind such that they'll remember it when they'll have grown up, you can rest easy, as they won't be able to remember it. Do you remember things from back when you were 18 to 24 months old? No, right?

The next step is easier. Once they have seen you going to the toilet, explain to them what you are doing so that they can understand. These include things such as removing your clothes while going to the toilet, flushing the commode, wiping, putting your clothes back on, washing your hands, and drying your hands. It'll get a little overwhelming for them if you try to explain it all at once, so be patient and take it one step at a time.

If the child sees the potty-training as something that they're already accustomed to, such as playing with their favorite toy or watching their favorite video on YouTube, they will be less daunted and more likely to look forward to going to the toilet. To that effect, make sure that at the beginning of the process, you have your child's potty somewhere familiar instead of the bathroom.

You can ask your child when they feel like their diaper is wet or full. Identify this behavior by asking them questions like, "Are you going to poop?" so your child can comprehend and recognize their urges to pee or poop.

Another thing you can do to prepare your child for potty training is keeping them in clean diapers. This requires you to be more attentive than usual, as you must replace their diapers within the window they dirty them. Once your child is accustomed to the feeling of cleanliness in their diapers, they will be mentally prepared to start potty-training.

Why Your Child's Having a Hard Time Potty-Training

It's crucial to understand that potty-training can be a very arduous task for your child, considering the number of changes they are going through. We are talking about their transition from diapers to the potty, their starting pre-school, moving from one place to the other, and learning all sorts of other things that aren't related to potty-training. This can overwhelm the child. It can cause unnecessary stress in their life. It might cause them to resist learning or straight up stop learning altogether. If your attempts at potty-training your toddler don't seem to work, here are reasons that will help you understand the why of it all. When you know the why, you can move on to the how. As in how to tackle those problems.

1. They are not Ready Yet

As much as we have discussed this, it needs to be reiterated at each stage of potty-training. Your child does not have control of their bladder and bowels before the age of 18 months, so teaching them potty-training before that time is not recommended. It will stall the progress and possibly cause complications that we shall discuss in the next section.

Listen, you might think that by putting your child on the potty every time they have to go—before they have turned 18 months old, that is—will train them, but it does not necessarily mean they are ready to go on their own. If you stop doing that, they will soil their diapers or pants. However, once after they've turned 18 months old, they will develop bladder and bowel control, and your training will pay off.

The not-being-ready-part is not limited to younger children. Sometimes, older children might have trouble because of being unready developmentally or medical issues, such as constipation.

Besides the physical and mental readiness, you must make sure that things are A-Okay at your house before you train them, specifically, in a familial capacity. Say you and your family are about to move, are planning to take a vacation or are about to have another baby. It might be better to wait because these changes signify new receptive learning for the child. When they are already too mentally occupied with other matters, it will not be the right time to potty-train them as their mental plates are already full.

Usually you can pick up on their lack of readiness through verbal and non-verbal cues. They will make faces, signifying displeasure and confusion and irritation, or they will tell you with their words and actions. If that persists, understand that they aren't ready and that they will be ready sometime later.

2. They Lack Interest

Think of the hundreds of different stimuli that your child is taking in at each moment. Imagine it from their perspective every little thing that their tiny little ears, ears, nose, mouth, hands, legs, and brain are witnessing, feeling, and assimilating. To say they are preoccupied with each of those stimuli wouldn't be an overstatement. We have to make a window for a teaching task, i.e., potty-training. If they do not pick up on it and instead give attention to other things, things such as the TV or their tablet or a gaming console, they are not to blame.

You are not to blame, either. This is a classic case of nobody's fault.

You have two options here. Either you can delay the potty-training till a time when they are less excited and antsy, or you can pique their interest in potty-training by including their favorite game, book, movie, or song in the mix. Understand that your child is not showing interest in the task because of some inborn rebellion or developmental disability; it's because there's too much going on their lives.

On a tangential note, the same goes for any other training. Whether you're teaching them how to speak, how to write, how to draw, or any other parental teaching task, if they cannot give their attention to the task at hand, it's because their little minds are overwhelmed with an overload of mental stimuli.

Some parents instruct their children in an environment where all other stimuli are zoned out, canceled. That's why they have a separate teaching room where there aren't any distractions. The same goes for potty-training.

3. They are Afraid of the Toilet

We've already covered this briefly, but now let's take another look from the perspective of your child having difficulty in adapting to potty-training. Your child knows when they are about to go to the bathroom. We discussed that. They will show their need to go either verbally or by nonverbal cues. So why would they rather dirty their diapers or their clothes instead of going to the bathroom? Well, it's because they're afraid of it. Again, it might be better to empathize and put yourself in your child's shoes. Look at the toilet. Look at it from their perspective. It's a huge porcelain chair with many moving parts, a huge height, and a giant hole in the middle, which flushes loudly. If they aren't afraid of the hole and the size, they might be afraid that they'll fall inside, and they'd be right to be afraid, as that has happened to many toddlers during their training. That's why it's recommended to use a training seat instead of just putting them on the plane seat.

Here are things that you can do to alleviate your child's fear of the toilet: Have them practice on the toilet by seating them on the toilet with their clothes still on. This way, you're familiarizing them with the toilet in a step by step manner. Put them on the toilet with the lid still on. This will help drive home the realization they aren't just going to fall inside. At this step, read their favorite book to them to distract them from the alien nature of the toilet. After your child can balance themselves on the closed toilet, you can lift up the lid and have them sit on it with their clothes on. Repeat that twice and then remove their clothes except the diaper. Last, have them sit on the toilet without the diaper and let them know that they have to go pee or poo. If your child resists at any step of the process, revert to the previous step so as not to overwhelm them.

This is why some parents prefer the potty to the toilet, as it helps familiarize the child without scaring them. Maybe your child fears the flushing of the toilet. There, you can explain to them the basics of how toilet plumbing works and demonstrate that working by having them flush a couple of toilet paper pieces.

4. They Do Not Want to Use a Public Toilet

This is a relatively rare case when you need to introduce your child to the public toilet, but since it happens lets cover it. Maybe you're traveling with your toddler and need to help them go to the toilet at a public toilet, or maybe they have to go to the toilet at their daycare or school. Regardless, sooner or later, your child must be introduced to the public toilet, which is a huge step for them, and as so, it will be scary for them. Scary as in they're afraid of the loud noises that emanate from the public toilet, noises such as the sound of flushing, people are talking, the hand dryer's loud whooshing, the opening, and closing of doors. While previously your child went to the toilet in the quiet comfort of their own home, now they're being made to go in a place that's altogether new and way too loud. Some public toilets have that auto-flush system, which can scare the child even more. If your child is resisting, it's recommended that you take a portable potty with you.

5. They are Anxious About Potential Accidents

This is a continuation of the last point. Suppose your child's potty-training is taking off at home, making you confident that they're able to use the toilet at a public place or at a friend or family member's home, and you introduce your child to a new toilet, you may notice that their displaying signs of nervousness. This is again due to the newness of the toilet. If the child is a little older, you can convey to them they can communicate their need to go, ask questions like "Where's the toilet," and express their need to go by saying, "I have to use the potty, please can you help me?"

Just in case, whenever you take your child out with you, pack a pair of clean clothes and diapers. This is for if or when they have an accident, you can help them regain their confidence by changing them into clean clothes quickly and letting them know that it's okay to have an accident.

6. They are Straight-Up Refusing to Potty-Train

Potty-training, both for you and your toddler, can be considered as the ultimate battleground. There are two methods of conflict. One's where you are pitted against your toddler, with the battlefield being that of potty-training. This is the bad kind of conflict. The other type of conflict, *the healthier one*, is where you and your toddler are in the same team, and potty-training's the opponent. In the former type of conflict, your child will become stubborn, and it will turn into a control issue.

Avoid that at all costs by being gentle with them and explaining it to them rationally that they can use the potty because now they are mature enough to do so. Be on their team; let them know that you're there for whenever they need assistance. Another thing you can do is provide them the illusion of control by giving them choices. Choose between two outfits, choose a TV program or a game on the tablet, choose what to eat, and so on. When they feel like they're somewhat in control, it will ease them into potty-training. It's vital to note there are three main things that your child can control: their need to eat and drink, their sleeping routine, and their toileting.

7. They Seem to be Slower than Your Other Child

We cannot stress enough that it is not a competition. Don't make it one. If your firstborn was quick to adapt to potty-train and your current child is seemingly having a tough time learning the ropes, it's not their fault. One method doesn't necessarily work for every child. Every child is different in their capacity to learn. One child may respond well to simple instructions; the other may respond well to rewards and positive affirmation.

Another significant difference that parents seem to overlook is the difference between potty-training boys and potty-training girls.

Some boys are slower to adapt to potty-training than some girls. It's not always the case, but it's not unheard of either.

Every child develops at their own pace. It doesn't mean they lack or excel in terms of their intelligence.

8. Their Health Issues are Aggravating and Interfering

Constipation is often the culprit to difficulties in potty-training. When a child is constipated, they'll fear going to the potty because of the pain associated with passing stool. Longtime constipation can cause complications by putting stool pressure on the child's kidneys and bladder, making it painful for them and difficult for them to go to the toilet.

It can aggravate into chronic constipation, which can cause encopresis, in which the stool becomes backed up and clogged with stool, and so, liquid stool leaks out. If you notice your child making accidents with leaky poop, consult with a pediatrician.

Constipation can be treated by having your child drink more water, introducing vegetables and fruits in your child's diet, and using a mild laxative.

Constipation also contributes to irritation and loss of appetite, thus interfering in the potty-training process.

Psychological Effects of Botched Potty-Training

If you, as a parent, give in to stress, it can cause things to go awry, turning the critical process of potty-training botched. If you feel like stress is getting the better of you, you can step back and give yourself some me-time. Relax. Take a deep breath. Get back in there with a fresh mind, because if you give in to your stress, you might lash out at your child or beat them, and that can have long-lasting effects.

Child Abuse

The American Academy of Pediatrics states that more child abuse takes place during potty-training compared to other facets of the child's development. If you hit your child or punish them during their training, it will lead to emotional and mental scarring that will stay with them for the rest of their lives. It will manifest itself in suicidal behavior, violent behavior, withdrawn behavior, depression, and it will make them prone to substance abuse when they are older.

Putting Pressure on Them with Your Expectations

By pressuring your child to perform, you will not only delay their learning process but also make them anxious and fearful. This can lead to fecal affecting by making them withhold their stool out of nervousness and being scared.

Punishing Them for Accidents

Scolding your child or punishing them for something as natural as an accident will give them low self-esteem, make them doubt their selves, and make them feel ashamed and embarrassed. The embarrassment will, in turn, lead to them hiding their need to go to the toilet. Once a child has associated potty-training with feelings of fear and shame, they will avoid it.

Preparing Yourself for Potty-Training

To avoid botching their potty-training, realize that more than your toddler, it is you who need to prepare yourself mentally for potty training. First, figure out your method early on and then stick to it. Once you've committed yourself to a potty-training method (which we'll discuss in detail later on), help your child get accustomed to it by being encouraging. Second, preparedness is everything. If you're mentally and resourcefully ready, it will be less taxing on your nerves. Third, take frequent breaks and allow yourself to detach from the whole parenting process for a little while. Hang out with your friends, go watch a movie, go to a bar, and just unwind. Fourthly, make some room for error so that when accidents do happen, you get to give yourself and your child some grace. Last, if you have more than one kid, do not compare one with the other, because there's only disappointment and confusion waiting for you there.

Now that we've covered the psychological basics of potty-training let's move on to using the potty for the first time.

Chapter Five: Using the Potty for the First Time

Congratulations on making it to this part of the book. It means that you've covered almost half the book, have understood the basics, and are now ready to take their toddler on their first potty-training run. We've broken down the task into detailed, easy-to-follow steps.

1. Picking Out the Potty

This is a step we have covered, but for revision's sake, we'll touch upon it just a little. As your toddler is now ready to be potty-trained, it's recommended that you pick out the potty with them, involving them in the process by considering what they are attracted to at the store. Taking your child shopping with you will serve two purposes: It will be a nice outing and bonding time for you and your child, and it will make them feel invested in the process by having a "choice," the choice is their selection of the potty. Use phrases like "Which one do you like more?" and consider the one they point at.

If they feel inclined towards more than one, splurge a little and get them two potties. They can serve as the main potty and the backup potty back at home. In the aisle where they sell potties, there will also be peripherals such as handles, splash guards, and toys. You can buy those. And buy snacks and treats for them so the trip to buying the potty becomes associated as a rewarding trip in their minds. You can, later, use those snacks and treats as a reward for when they've gone on the potty for the first time.

2. Acquainting Them with the Potty

Now that you have shopped for the potty and have selected one suitable for your child, it's time to acquaint them with the potty at home. This differs from their picking out the potty at the store, where their curiosity and sense of wonder were piqued by the array of choices they had. Now that you have come home, that same curiosity might be replaced by them overlooking the potty. You know how kids are in terms of their attention spans.

Acquainting them with the potty at home can be done by putting the potty in the living room or their bedroom or in the toilet, and establishing to your toddler this is the new place to go potty, should they need to go.

Right now, you need not worry about getting them out of their diapers right away, as they have yet to go to on the potty for the first time. But it might be useful to notice how long they are staying dry between their peeing and pooping intervals. If they are dry for over two hours, it's time to acquaint them with the potty. Reinforce the words "poop and "pee" with the potty, so they are at least aware that that's' where they need to go. Since the potty hasn't been used yet and is clean, you can let your child play with it, sparking their sense of wonder.

3. Informing Them that Their Training has Started

Once the potty has been bought, and your child has acquainted themselves with it, it's time to have a one-on-one session with them where you tell them that their potty-training has begun. Make sure that you do not use advance or complex terms but instead use phrasing that they will be able to comprehend, such as "Now we're going to use the potty to go pee or poo, okay?" Select a phrasing and stick to it throughout the training. If you want to refer to their urine as pee and their stool as poo, that's okay. In fact, that's recommended.

For your own convenience, you can put up a chart to log in the hours they stay dry, when they went to potty, and when did they dirty their diapers, and so on. You can involve your child in this process by explaining to them what the rows and columns in the chart stand for. You can ask them if they have any questions, and then you can answer them when they ask you.

It's even better if you can watch a YouTube how-to video with them to engage them more thoroughly in the process. If your child is more of a reader, there are plenty of books on going to the potty for the first time you can read with them.

4. Having a Dry Run at the Potty

Once you and your child have communicated about the commencement of their potty-training, it's time to take them on a dry run. This is where you ask them to sit on the potty with their clothes and diapers still on. Once you have introduced them to the potty and have explained its function to them, invite them or request them politely to sit on it and don't make a grandiose thing of it right away. First, just have them sit on it ask them how it feels. They'll try to tell you what they're feeling and experiencing and will ask you question about the big hole in the middle, or the potty's handles, shape, or color. Entertain their questions with humor and tell them they have to use the potty from now on. See what their reaction is to this added information. Notice how they respond. If they respond affirmatively, it means you're good to go and can continue with the next steps of the training. If, however, they throw a tantrum or displaying negative emotions, it might be better to pause here and retry later on when they're more receptive and in the mood to interact with the potty.

5. Sticking to a Potty-Training Method

There are four main potty-training methods you can stick to. There aren't just four; it varies for each kid on a child to child basis. Let's discuss the methods.

- **Parent-led potty-training.** In this method, you, as the parent, stick to a certain schedule. One or more partners or caregivers can participate in this method, making it easier for the more people. You will allot the time for your child's toileting. The advantage of this method is that there's no need to shift your schedule massively to train your child. You can just fit everything in your timetable, provided you're consistent. The con of this method is that since you are leading the method, your child might ignore or overlook their bodily instincts altogether, relying on you to take them to the potty every time.

- **Infant potty-training.** In this potty-training method, you train your child in their infancy, i.e., one month to four months. The pro of this method is that you save a ton of money on diapers by not introducing them to your child from the start. The disadvantage is this method is very messy. In this method, you will keep an eye on your child's body signals to see when they have to go, and then you sit them down on the potty. It might require you to be intuitive, this method.

- **3-day potty-training.** We have discussed this method before in potty-training boot-camp.

- **Child-led potty-training.** In this method, you let your child adapt to the toilet on their own, not pushing or pointing them to the toilet, instead of explaining to them that when they have to go pee or poo, they should use the toilet, and then letting them adapt to it at their own pace.

This list is by no means exhaustive but covers general methods that parents use.

6. Assisting Them on their First Time

Now that we have stuck to a method, it's time to assist them on their first run at the potty. There's going to be some confusion on their end, but that's normal. First, take your child's pants off, then their diaper, and tell them to go sit on the toilet. Do this only when your intuition tells you they are about to relieve themselves. They will ask you some questions as to why they must sit on it instead of relieving themselves in their diapers. This is an excellent opportunity to explain the transition to them in terms they understand.

Once they are seated on the potty, stay with them, and tell them to let go or let loose. That they have to push to relieve themselves, this might be tricky for their first time, but if they get the hang of it, it will pay off. They might look confused, but that's natural. Tell them that there's no pressure on them, and there's no rush. If they cannot go, you can pause and repeat it later, when they are well fed and need to go.

It might do them good to distract them by way of a toy or a story since they already have a habit of going in their diapers while they are occupied with doing whatever they're doing in their regular routine. So, think of their sitting on the potty as them just sitting on a regular chair, and tell them that too in terms they will understand.

Hold their hand and gently squeeze it to set on the peristalsis that will eventually cause them to poop. Ask them if they are feeling pressure doing there, and if so, then they should relax and let it go.

This is the most critical part and should be taken as such.

7. Affirming Them after the First Time

Now that they have gone successfully their first time, it's time to reaffirm them by praising them and letting them know that they have done a good job. Give them a treat of their favorite candy or snack to let them know that they succeeded. But note that you should not make it a habit. This is for the first time only, and occasionally on every fifth or tenth successful potty session to keep them on the right track.

Explain to them that their going on the potty for the first time was an accomplishment. Kiss them, hug them, and smile at them. An excited "woohoo!" will go a long way in affirming them.

Say encouraging phrases like "You did a good job!" and "I'm so proud of you!" They won't be able to understand exactly what you're saying, but they'll pick up on the phrasing and the manner it is uttered in, thereby understanding they did something right.

8. Introducing Cleaning Methods

We are not done yet. There's still the cleaning to do. Now, since this was their first time on the potty, they cannot be expected to clean themselves on their own. You will have to assist them. Some parents decide on having their child clean themselves up right off the bat while other parents clean them up on their first few attempts. Decide on what you want to do beforehand.

If you want them to clean themselves, introduce them to toilet paper or wet wipes. For children with sensitive skin, wet wipes are a better option as they reduce the chances of rashes. For normal skin, toilet paper is how to go. For boys, teach them to wipe from back to front. For girls, it's front to back to avoid and UTIs.

If they have only peed, teach them to shake it off if they're a boy, and for girls to teach them to wipe themselves with a wipe or toilet paper.

Once they are completely clean, inform them of the importance of cleaning after going on the potty. Besides your teaching, you can play a video that explains it. There are a plethora of toddler-friendly YouTube videos that do that for you.

9. Emptying the Potty

After they have cleaned up, it's time to reinforce this part of the process but not aggressively or forcefully. It should be like presenting the casual as causal. Take the filled potty, making sure that your child is properly cleaned and is standing by as an observer, and explain to them that that contents of the potty go in the "grown-up toilet." Then, you can make it more interactive for them by having them look at the emptied contents and pushing the flush button or lever. Notice how their interest gets piqued as they see the water taking away all the contents. Ask them how that felt. Did that feel good? Do they want to do it again? If it's a hearty yes, that's good. That means they are already looking forward to the next session.

Once they have flushed, you can show them how to flush an empty toilet all over again and explaining to them the plumbing mechanics in a toddler-friendly tone. "The pipes take the poo-poo and pee-pee away."

Tell them they did a good job flushing the toilet, and that they should now move on to the next step, washing their hands.

10. Post-Potty Follow-Up

The post-potty follow up can be broken down into two steps. One: Washing their hands and explaining the importance of hygiene to them. Two: Putting their clothes back on.

The first part will be tedious for the child, as they have allotted quite a lot of time into the first potty-session, and now they are antsy to get back into their regular routine. So, you'll notice a bit of rebellion as the child tries to run away out of the bathroom. Some might be over-eager to wash their hands, mimicking the behavior they have observed in their parent. You can make things interesting for them by using a kid-friendly, bubbly soap that creates many colorful bubbles and foam. Teach them the proper way of washing their hands and drying them off with a towel.

Now you may put their clothes back on. Notice how the child feels reacquainted with a sense of normalcy once they have their clothes back on and are heading out of the bathroom, free from their training. At this time, you should not put their diaper back on. That's the next step. Just observe how your child goes about diaperless and relieved about the house. What are they doing? Make a mental note in your head.

11. Putting their Diaper Back On

If you are following the three-day potty-training method, you might want to skip this step as this step sort of sets you back a bit in terms of the time-frame for the potty-training.

If, however, you're following the parent-led potty-training method, you should observe your kid for at least an hour and a half. During this time, if they have to go to the toilet again you should take them to the potty again. If they are dry, you should take a breather and put their diaper back on to give yourself some break and letting them reacquaint with their familiar method of relieving themselves.

Avoid pull-up pants, as they tend to halt the process of the potty-training, as we have discussed.

After you have put their diaper back on, tell your toddler why you have done so. It is for emergencies only. When they want to go again, they should tell you. Don't expect them to stick this instruction, which is why we are putting diapers on them in the first place, i.e., for room of mistakes. And considering that it was their first time on the potty, there should be a lot of room for mistakes. As with most habits, they shall perfect it the more they practice.

12. Checking the Diaper for Dryness

After putting their diaper back on, watch their behavior throughout the day—more specifically, every two hours—and check on their diaper in that time to gauge how long they stay dry. If they are keeping dry for two or over two hours, it means they are ready to continue with the routine. If, on the other hand, they aren't remaining dry for two hours, do not worry as this is just the beginning of their potty-training. In the following week they will start picking up on preferring the potty instead of their diapers, which is when we ditch the diapers altogether.

13. Asking for their Feedback

After their first potty session, ask your child how they felt, what they liked, what they disliked, what they want to do again, and if they think they are ready to keep on using the potty in place of the diaper. Ask these questions in a way that doesn't patronize them or downplay the importance of their potty-training.

14. Sticking to a Plan

Congratulations on your first successful potty session with your toddler. This is the ripe time for making a plan and sticking to it for the next week or however long the training takes. It's critical that you stick to that plan throughout their training.

15. Repeating All of the Above

Does that sound a bit hectic? Well, it is. You have to repeat the above steps several times throughout their training. This will be a test of your patience and your resilience. It will also be an opportunity for your child to learn of the training, and that comes with its own fair share of growing pains. But since you're sticking to a plan, remaining rational throughout, and giving yourself frequent breaks, it will not be an insurmountable problem as much as it will be a manageable routine.

Chapter Six: Potty and Pooping Problems

The domain of potty training comes with its own problems. These problems can complicate the training process, making it both irritating for you as the parent and for your child as the learner. Let's discuss some major problems that might arise in training and come up with solutions for each one of them.

1. No peeing; Only Pooping

If you notice that your child is only pooping and not peeing when they use the potty, do not worry. This is only natural. In the case of some children, they develop their bowel control before they can develop their bladder control. This manifests by them only pooping and not peeing. It also manifests in the form of them wetting their diapers and the bed at night. This isn't a cause for alarm. The solution to this problem is relatively simple and does not require you to do a lot. You have only to continue with the potty-training as usual and clean the mess and swap their diapers for new ones whenever they pee involuntarily.

2. Playing with their Poop

Children are inquisitive by nature, and their inquisitive can show in them trying to play with their poop in the potty's bowl. They might try to grab it, hold it in their hand and fling it, or simply try to smell it. When that happens, you have to be stern with them, but not aggressively so. Reassert to them that poop is not meant to be played with. It's waste, it's smelly, and it dirties your hands when you touch it. Tell them that and see how they respond. If they still persist wanting to play with their poop, switch them to the adult potty with a seat so that they cannot reach their poop.

3. Your Son Sits Down to Pee

You should start training your son to stand up to pee from the start. If you notice that he wants to sit down to pee, it is a problem, but not one that cannot be tackled. Your solution to this problem should be to let your child sit down and pee at the beginning, and after they have mastered their bladder control, describe to them they have to stand up while peeing. If you're a mother trying to get him to stand up while peeing, it might be better to let their dad or one of their male caregivers to help them with the peeing process.

4. Resistance is Futile

Is your child resisting going to the potty? This might be because of a power struggle, which we have covered extensively in the previous sections. Maybe they are resisting because they are not ready yet, which is another point that we have covered thoroughly. When you see them resisting, revert to the previous step, i.e., diapers, and let them have a few days before you get back to training them. This time around, after you have communicated the importance of going to the potty, they will be less resistant and more open to the idea of using the potty.

5. Accidents

Accidents will happen. Brace yourself for that beforehand, and you will save yourself a lot of mental and physical toll. Be ready for whenever accidents happen with cleaning supplies and a fresh change of clothes. Sometimes your child might not want to go to the potty and isn't wearing a diaper either, which will result in them pooping on the floor or peeing somewhere in the living room. It is not recommended to scold or punish your child for any accidents that they cause. Punishment will make them feel ashamed and guilty and embarrassed and even rebellious.

6. Being Upset Over Flushing

Some children treat their poop and pee as part of their bodies, thinking that since they came out of their bodies, the poop and the pee are something that they should hold on to instead of flushing them, which will cause them becoming upset when you flush the toilet. It might cause them to throw a tantrum and cry, and the absolute worst-case scenario is that they will try to reach for the material being flushed. You must stop them if they try the latter. In terms of explaining to them that it is okay to flush, you can try telling them that their poop and pee are smelly and dirty and that they should be gotten rid of by flushing. If at first, they appear to be confused, that's okay. They will pick up on it in time.

7. Fear of the Toilet

While some children might be over-eager to go to the toilet, others will exhibit fear and anxiety and nervousness when using the toilet. This is exactly why we opted for a potty, as it is manageable and smaller and something that they won't be afraid of. Remember, it's a step by step process, and using the toilet comes at the end of it, not at the beginning. So, if you notice your toddler being nervous about the toilet, shift them to the potty and stick to it until you are certain that they aren't afraid anymore. It might do them good if you asked them to vocalize their fears so that you could alleviate them.

8. Wanting a Diaper When They Want to Poop

Your child is still coming to terms with using the potty, and so it is natural that they want to use a diaper when they want to poop.

This will be a bit confusing for you, as you'll have already taught them to use the potty, so why do they want to go back to the diaper to poop? The answer is familiarity. They have been familiar with relieving themselves on their diapers for so long that instead of choosing the potty right away, they'll stick with the diapers. There's no cause to be frustrated at this, as with subsequent sessions, they shall start using the potty more often and grow less reliant on the diapers, and eventually will not use the diapers at all. If that sounds like a fantasy right now, trust in the training and believe that they shall outgrow their need for diapers very soon.

9. Pooping in a Specific Place Other than the Toilet

This is more of a continuation of the last point. Have you noticed that your child goes to a specific place in the house when they display signs of wanting to pee or poop? Where do they go? Do they hide behind the sofa or the curtains? Do they squat in front of the TV in the lounge and make straining faces? When you put the potty in front of them, do they resist sitting on it and instead try to revert to their previous mode of relieving? If so, there's an easy fix for that. Follow them to where they go to relieve themselves and put their potty there and ask them to go on it. Take their clothes off and put them on the potty in their familiar place and repeat that till they have become more acclimatized to the potty rather than their familiar places.

10. Bedwetting

Even though we'll cover bedwetting in the nighttime potty-training section, let's consider it for now as a potty-training problem and discuss how you can help your toddler in stopping bedwetting. Children take a long time to complete their nighttime training. More than daytime potty-training. That's because nighttime potty-training comes with its own set of challenges. The most important thing that you can do as their parent or guardian is have them go to the potty before they go to sleep, minimize the amount of liquid they consume before going to bed, and make sure that they use the potty right after they have woken up. If you want to avoid bedwetting instantly, it might be wise to use diapers for a few days until you have started their nighttime training. You can convey to them that they should inform you if they wake up during the night with the urge to go. This will require you to be on alert when they are sleeping since if they have understood what you said to them, they will come to you when they need to go, and if you're sleeping when they come to you, they'll create a mess.

11. They Only Poop or Pee Right After They've Been on the Potty

This is probably the most frustrating of the potty-training problems, and you are not to blame if you feel irritated when this happens. You sat your child down on the potty and expected them to go on it, but instead of using it, they stay dry and only go right after you pull them off the potty. They might make a mess on the floor or in their clothes. This will get jarring for you, irritating even, and you'll ask yourself why this is happening. It is happening because of pressure. They feel like they're being pressurized to perform, and being unable to do so, they make a mess. If this happens, you can either delay the potty-training until they have stopped doing this, or you can bear through the mess they make and stick to seating them down on the potty and staying with them while they try to relieve themselves.

12. They Only Go to the Potty with a Specific Person

Are there multiple caregivers at your house, besides you and your partner? Do people like your child's aunt or uncle or grandparents or a nanny? Does your child only go to the potty with a specific person? This isn't exactly a problem as much as it is a matter of your child's comfort. They are comfortable in going to the toilet with a specific person. If you want them to go to the potty with you, here are a couple of things you can try: reacquaint yourself with your toddler if for the past couple of days you feel like you have been distant with them; stay with them as they use the potty with the person they are comfortable with; and then, finally, remove the person till it's only you and the toddler on the potty.

13. Going Back to Diapers

Do you feel like your child is reverting to their diapers after having a successful run at the potty a couple of times? Try pinpointing the changes in the environment that might be causing them to revert. Are they undergoing stress? Is the potty-training routine too rigorous for them? Is there a communication gap between you and your child? Are they unable to go on the potty? Try finding the root cause of why they want to use the diapers and eliminate that cause rather than putting them back on diapers. However, if the mess-making persists, you might want to pause the potty-training right there and revert them to the diapers for the time being.

14. Hiding When They Make a Mess

Your child will hide behind furniture more often if they are making a mess somewhere in the house other than in their diapers or on the potty. Finding the mess is the easier part of this problem. You have only to follow your nose. Dealing with the child is the hard part. You will be tempted to reprimand them, but that will not be beneficial either for you or your child. You can sit them down and talk to them and try to understand what they are going through. They will try to tell you what they are feeling, and as nonsensical as their jumbled-up words sound like, it's crucial that you listen to them and try to ascertain the underlying problem. Is it confidence, or the lack of it? Is it because they have an upset stomach? Or have you possibly started the training a little too early, and they're not ready yet?

How You Can Solve Some of These Potty-Training Problems

If you are facing any of the mentioned problems—or worse, many of them at the same time—it is only natural that you have felt frustrated with the lack of progress in your training. Let's go over some methods you can apply in your training to make things easier for you and your toddler.

Reverse Psychology

More specifically: Pretending like you do not care. Does this sound a little too cold? Well, it need not be. You are not expected to become so aloof that your child starts craving for your attention. But you have to pretend like you're not too frustrated by the hitch in their training. It will take some of the pressure off your child and let them get reacquainted with their routine. Once they are back in their comfort zone, they will start to take potty-training a bit more candidly. Why does reverse psychology work? It's because some children have a knack for saying no to whatever you propose to them. It's not something they do on purpose; rather, it's an essential part of their growing up. It has nothing to do with how you have been training them so far. It's just that they have learned an unfamiliar word, i.e., "no," and are just now getting to understand its connotations.

An example of reverse psychology would be you telling them that if they haven't gone to the potty yet, it's completely okay. This way, you will not have to take them to the park and can stay home all day. Now, in this scenario, if your child really loves going to the park, they'll start thinking, "Oh no, I really wanted to go to the park, and now we're not going." After doing this once or twice, notice how they go to the potty on their own. Potty-training reverse psychology is an excellent tool to have at your disposal. If it makes you feel a bit evil, well, don't. You're dealing with a toddler here, and excluding punishment and reprimanding, everything goes here.

Cutting Back on Their Rewards

If you started giving your child rewards every time they used the potty, there's a good chance that you have done something Pavlovian. They now associate going to the potty with the reward they will get, and whenever you do not offer them a reward, they'll get antsy and irritated and will be unable to use the potty.

If this is the case, consider scaling back on their rewards and getting back into the training without a lot of hurrah and here-you-go involved. Consider this: They aren't always going to get a reward every time they go use the potty. Are you possibly spoiling them with way too many rewards? This might be unintentional, as giving them the promise of rewards if they successfully go to the potty can be an appealing, easy fix for a problem that seems to have no solution at the moment.

By cutting down on their rewards and reasserting that they have to go on the potty, you'll be better able to deal with their Pavlovian desire to have a treat every time they use the potty.

This also holds true for stars and colors that go on their potty-training chart. At some point, you have to scale back on the celebratory nature of their potty usage. It's better if it's sooner than later.

Fixing Their Constipation Issues

Sometimes it's not because of your child's moods they aren't able to use the potty as much as it is about their physical incapability to use it. Case in point—constipation. Notice if the child is crankier than usual and is always on edge whenever it's potty time. Are they grunting and straining more than usual? If so, it might be that they are constipated. Introduce high-fiber foods in their diets, such as green vegetables and whole-grain bread, to help them with their constipation. Be careful, though, as introducing more than the recommended dose of high-fiber foods in their diet will have a negative effect on their stomach's health.

Is Your Child Testing You?

A child's cognitive growth allows them to understand your patterns and test the limits you have imposed on them. This might come off as rebellion to us grownups, but for a child, these little acts of rebellions ("No" in response to a request you made, throwing tantrums when you try to force them to do something, and throwing stuff around the house in anger) make perfect sense. But you aren't expected to stand by idly either. Be firm about the limits that you have set up and stick to them, regardless of their throwing a tantrum or straight-up refusing. You're the adult here, not them. You know what's better for your child, not them. Here, again, reverse psychology can come into play and make them think that they've got control instead of you. Once that has been asserted, they'll want to go to the toilet on their own. Whether or not they are testing you or not, the fact remains that sooner or later, they have to use the potty.

Chapter Seven: Nighttime Potty Training

Nighttime potty-training is in a whole different ballpark of its own, requiring a separate, detailed chapter where we will cover the basics, some tips, and the time it shall take your toddler to be trained. Let's get right into it.

Difference Between Daytime and Nighttime Potty-Training

There are several differences between daytime and nighttime potty-training, the most marked one being their different bowel and bladder movements. Of course, your child has by now gotten a little control over their bladder and bowels. You can observe this by their daytime potty-training habits, but what about nighttime? Well, nighttime training requires them to have more control over these two muscles than daytime because they lose voluntary control while they are sleeping. You might notice this in the form of bedwetting and even pooping while they are asleep. This is no cause for alarm or worry. This is exactly why we are covering nighttime training. A potty-training expert, Samantha Allen, says that potty-training is a daytime process and that you cannot be expected to teach someone something when they have lost consciousness, i.e., when they are sleeping. You can, however, she adds, set your kid up to successfully stay dry during the night.

Remember that nighttime training requires a lot of developmental prerequisites, the most important one being control over their muscles. Subconscious control. Your child might be excelling at their daytime potty-training, but they'll be able only to successfully train for nighttime when they have covered a few developmental milestones. Another important milestone that they need to cover is their eating and drinking habits. Last, it's the hormone that suppresses urine production at night that is the most crucial factor in their nighttime training. If the production of that hormone has not started yet, their training cannot be complete. If you try to persevere through that phase—without the assistance of the hormone—you are going to impact the child's self-esteem and confidence, making them confused and irritated. It will make them dread going to the toilet.

Nighttime potty-training happens way later than daytime potty-training. Unless your child has mastered all elements of daytime potty-training, they cannot be expected to excel in nighttime potty-training.

When to Start Nighttime Potty-Training

Consider nighttime potty-training once your child displays signs of readiness. Some signs of readiness to look out for include:

1. Seeing that their diaper is warm when they wake up. If it is cold, they are not ready for nighttime potty-training. The warm diaper signifies that your child is wetting their diaper after they have woken up. A cold diaper suggests that they went sometime during the night when they were asleep. Additionally, notice if their diaper has poop in it when they wake up. Normally it should not have

poop in it, but if there are signs, it might be better to hold off the training till their diapers are void of poop. Remember, this is not the child's fault since their bodies are undergoing involuntary, unconscious motions when they are asleep.

2. Once you have ascertained that their diapers are warm and wet instead of cold and wet, the next sign to look out for readiness is checking to see how frequently their diapers are dry when they wake up in the morning. If their diapers are frequently dry, it means that they have started getting control of their bladder while they are asleep. This might be because of the hormone production or because their bladder has strengthened. In both cases, it is a major win.

3. The last step to look out for in terms of readiness is your child asking that you remove their diaper or nappies when they want to sleep. This signifies that they are confident that they won't wet the bed while asleep. This also signifies their want for independency. Again, in both cases, this is a major win as you have progressed beyond all three signs and are now ready to teach your toddler nighttime training.

If you want further clarification in terms of whether they are ready or not, ask yourself these questions: Is your child able to follow simple directives? Are they physically able to go to the bathroom? Can they get on the potty or the toilet on their own? Are they staying dry for longer than two hours? If the answer to most of those questions is yes, your child is ready for nighttime potty-training. If all the signs of readiness are there, it's better that you start their nighttime training sooner than later since if you delay the process, it might cause complications with their daytime training. The typical age for nighttime training is between 2 years to 3 years. Ideally, if the child has gone a few weeks with no incidents, it's best to commence their training.

How Long Does Nighttime Potty-Training Last?

It's only natural to wonder how long this training shall last, as you'll already have mastered daytime training by now. Well, most children can get through an entire night by the age of four to five. Bedwetting, however, is going to persist a little longer till after they are five since it is a developmental deficiency rather than one concerned with chronological age. If you have a daughter, you will notice that there's going to be a slight difference between training her and training a son. It isn't that big of a difference, but for clarification's sake, we shall cover it at length in the next chapter.

You can expect nighttime training to last for around one to two months, as there's going to be a lot of nights where inconsistencies occur, some nights where they wet the bed, some weeks where they won't even get it once. It's a lot to take in, which is why we have prepared some tips that you can follow to make sure everything goes smoothly. Again, here patience is the biggest virtue that will see you through this part of their training. Patience and empathy. Understand that nighttime training is relatively harder than daytime training and that your toddler is doing all they can to learn the ropes.

Tips You Can Follow

If you want to ditch the overnight diapers, follow these tips to make sure that your child is getting the most out of their nighttime training.

1. Setting Up a Consistent Daytime Training Plan

The success of nighttime training depends upon the consistency of daytime training. Both of them are directly proportional. Once it has been a few weeks—or better yet, a month and a half—you can start their nighttime training. The potty-training plan for their daytime training must be individualized to suit your child. It's not a one-schedule-fits-all kind of deal.

Let's go over the basics of daytime potty-training: They stay dry for two or more hours, they have started using the potty on their own, they can pull off their clothes and put them on once they are done, and they can wash their hands.

Now consider how that affects their nighttime training. Once you have started, let them know that they should go to the potty once before they are going to sleep, and once during the middle of the night when they wake up. You can communicate this with them in easy-to-follow, simple directives that do not boggle or confound them. Don't expect them to follow these steps right off the bat. It will take some time. Meanwhile, keep on training them in daytime training irrespective of the progress of their nighttime training. Their confidence in their daytime training will play a key role in their nighttime training.

2. Taking Your Family History

If your parents are available to talk to, you should ask them how long it took you to potty-train both in the daytime and in the nighttime. Ask them about the methods they used to train you, what worked for them and what didn't work for them. Ask them about the age that you stopped wetting the bed, the age at which you went to the potty without their assistance, and the age at which you ditched your diapers. It shall be a little nostalgic walk down the memory lane, and an excellent opportunity for you to learn about your history. Later, you can use that knowledge to your advantage by implementing it in your child's life

Kids take after their parents, and not just in matters of their appearance. They emulate the same habits, the same taste in things, and the same dislikes. Knowing about yourself will give you an insight into the behavior of your toddler in an altogether new way. This isn't limited to just you. Encourage your partner to ask their parents about their history. To expand the information pool, you can ask your uncles and aunts about their experiences with your cousins.

Accidents such as bedwetting run in the family. Knowing whether or not you used to wet the bed will inform you about the child's tendencies.

3. Limiting their Liquid Intake

To prevent nighttime bedwetting, the most recommended route is limiting your child's liquid intake after the evening. Ideally, you should not let them drink anything after dinner. But this is not a hard and fast rule, as your child is bound to feel thirsty sometime after dinner. The easy fix to that is getting one of those brightly colored plastic shot glasses. Filling them with water or milk or juice will not only quench your child's thirst, but it shall make them feel like they have drunk a substantial amount of liquid because they will see the glass as full and not its small size.

Sugary liquids are a hard no after dinner, as these tend to fill up the bladder with more water as compared to plain water.

In any case, you should not introduce your child to soft drinks that early on. It's not good for their teeth – as well as their health. If your child is lactose intolerant, they're bound to make a mess in bed if you feed them milk. The water that you give them at dinner and after dinner should not be too cold, as chilly water also induces the need to urinate.

4. Make Them Use the Potty Before They Go to Bed and After They Wake Up

Once you have decided on potty-training your child in the nighttime, you must have them go to the potty at least once before they go to bed. Ideally, you should have them go on the potty half an hour before bedtime. On a tangential note, this is an excellent opportunity to form the habit of nighttime brushing. But since it's just their milk teeth, it's okay if they don't pick the habit of nighttime brushing right away. You can be lenient in that regard.

Take them to the potty first thing after they have woken up and have them sit on it for a few minutes to empty their bladder and bowel. Again, this is an excellent time to get them in the habit of brushing their teeth after waking up. The sooner they pick up on that habit, the better.

Notice the consistency of their potty routine before and after they wake up. If they are sticking to it regularly, it means that their nighttime potty-training is progressing at a good pace. Now might be the time to pat yourself on the back for a job well done, but not too hard a pat, as we're not out of the training routine yet.

5. Preparing for Potential Accidents

Nighttime potty-training accidents are considerably different from daytime ones, the most prominent and irritating problem—both for you and your toddler—being bedwetting. In this case, you should prepare by double layering the sheets, using a plastic sheet under those sheets to make sure that the wetness doesn't soak up in the mattress, and keeping a spare change of clothes, diapers, and sheets at hand should they wet the bed. A very thorough method to counter bedwetting includes adding a waterproof protector, a sheet on top of that, then another layer of waterproof protector, and last, another sheet on top of that. When they do wet the bed, you can strip off the two layers on top and not have to worry about changing the two sheets below. If you're looking for a quick fix, consider adding pee pads under the sheets.

6. Should You Wake Them Up in the Night, or Not?

This is the big one. Should you or shouldn't you wake them up during the night? Some parents who are rigorous about the nighttime training wake up their child whether or not their child is a deep sleeper. That is not recommended, as by waking up the child who's a light sleeper, you'll disturb the rest of their sleep cycle, thereby making them irritated and vexed unnecessarily. Only wake your child up in the night if you're certain that they can fall asleep easily once they're done using the potty. However, if it feels exhausting after the first few attempts, you can skip this part of the training and move on to the next one, as this isn't as crucial to their nighttime training as the other steps.

7. Checking their Dryness Patterns

Keep a vigilant check on how long they stay dry for after they have woken up, and if their diapers are dry at all right after they wake up. If their diapers are remaining dry for a week, it's time to skip them altogether and try making them sleep without diapers or pull-up pants.

8. Following their Lead

In the case of one parent, their five-year-old son started telling them that he was ready for nighttime training. The parent did not ask their son, nor did they push him in any way. The child-initiated the nighttime training because he wanted to be dry in his bed.

Take note from that example and try to follow your child's lead. They're in tune with their body, as much as a child can be, and sometimes they know better when to start. Do not force them or try to get them jump-started as this will—as we have mentioned numerous times—aggravate the problem instead of solving it.

9. Celebrating the Little Things

Once they have progressed to keeping the bed and their diapers dry for a week or so, celebrate this milestone with them by giving them their favorite treat, watching a movie with them, or taking them toy shopping.

10. Understanding the Cause

There might be an underlying cause to their bedwetting. It can be a health issue. If you notice them consistently wetting the bed, take them to a pediatrician and discuss what the problem might be.

It might be uneven hormone production or a weak bladder. In either case, the doctor shall prescribe you medication and a dietary regimen to follow.

Chapter Eight: Potty Training Girls vs. Boys

Potty-training, a girl, differs from training a boy. Regardless, it's a challenge in both cases. Let's look at the distinct differences between training a girl and a boy.

Boys Take a Little Longer to Train

Boys do not show interest in using the potty in the beginning. Girls, in comparison, are more receptive to it. Because of that, boys are slower to master potty-training. The myth that boys are longer to train than girls originates from here. This isn't exactly true. The time frame for both their training is almost the same. It's just that boys start a little later. In terms of completing the training, the approximate time stays the same regardless of their gender. In a poll of 1300 moms that was conducted by Made for Moms, it was found that roughly 56 percent of girls were potty-trained by the age of 2-1/2 months, while only 44 percent of boys were trained by that age. While this isn't exactly a big difference, if you are a diaper-buying parent, this small difference can seem longer in terms of the economics of it all.

Boys Have to Learn Two Different Ways of Going

Boys have to learn how to stand up to pee and then sit down to poop while girls only have to learn how to sit down. Some parents teach their boys to stand up first and then sit on the potty later. Other parents do the opposite; they teach their sons to sit down and do both poop and pee on the potty and then teach them how to stand up and pee. The tricky part is teaching them to aim their pee in the toilet such that it does not cause splashes. If you are teaching them to pee while standing up, only move on to them sitting down once they have mastered peeing standing up, and where you are teaching them to sit down, only move on to standing up once they have mastered sitting down. Of course, the rules with pooping are different. The previous instructions are for peeing only. When it comes to pooping, both boys and girls have the same method, i.e., sitting down. They may even pee during their pooping session, which is only natural and should be encouraged.

Girls Mature Faster than Boys

This isn't a myth. Girls, indeed, develop faster than boys in terms of intelligence and physiology. Girls also develop language skills faster than boys, which allows them to understand your instructions quicker, thus making it easier to potty-train them. Girls also learn how to take their dresses off and put them on faster than boys, and gain control of their bladder and bowel faster than boys, all of which makes it easier to train them. But note that the period for the training remains the same for both boys and girls.

Now let's make a side-by-side comparison for boys and girls in various stages of their potty-training.

Potty-Training Commencement Based on their Gender

Although the *when* of it all depends upon the individual child more than any pre-existing guideline, the gender of the child can play a huge role in deciding when to start their training.

Boys: Boys will take their time in being developmentally ready to start potty-training. Thus, their training will be delayed as compared to girls. How delayed, you ask? Well, a few months give or take. The factors that decide on their readiness include their interest in potty-training, the development of their bowel and bladder control, and their routine. Most parents who are training their boys say that they start teaching them at the age of two.

Girls: Girls are quicker to adapt to potty-training early on. They will manifest this by showing interest in going to the potty. If you have a girl, you can start training her at the age of 18 months. Before that, they will not be completely ready.

While these are the approximate times to start their training, remember that for each child, the case is different, regardless of their gender, where some are early adopters, other moderate learners, and some slow to learning potty-training. To see if they are ready for potty-training, consult the first chapter in the book to see the signs of their readiness.

One other difference in choosing when to start potty-training the child is their choice of distraction. Girls tend to be more on the reserved side in most cases, relying on subtler toys and music and movies to distract themselves. In contrast, boys are a little rowdier, relying on louder toys, louder videos, and videogames to keep themselves occupied. This is yet another reason why girls pick up on potty-training than boys, as they aren't as distracted with their playtime as boys are. Boys are more preoccupied with their toys and games and movies, and so can be tricky when teaching them how to use the potty.

Adjusting Potty-Training Techniques for the Child Based on their Gender

If you are a parent to more than one child, you may have seen that your older child was quite different to train than your younger one. If the older child was a girl, then she might have taken less time to train. If it was a boy, he might have taken more time to train. You have to remember to change and try different techniques for potty-training, and sometimes, you must come up with a customized technique you haven't used before.

Boys: Boys will sit on the potty, go, and then get up and say that they are finished. They won't be concerned with cleaning themselves up right away. Also, when it comes to wiping, for boys, this is not a big concern, as they can both wipe back to front and front to back.

Girls: But girls must wipe front to back, or else they will contract bacterial infections in their vagina. Girls will also be quicker to adapt to the potty as they'll want to be a "big girl" badly.

Ten Gender-Specific Tips to Help Your Toddler

Tip #1

Girls: Choosing Size-Appropriate Seats

Buying a potty that's smaller and compact is recommended for your girl. This will reduce the chances of splashing while peeing, and the chances of them falling inside it. Boys tend to need bigger potties than girls. For us, our adult-sized toilet might seem very normal and manageable in size but think of it from your daughter's perspective. It's a goliath porcelain throne!

Boys: Getting the Green Light

If you start training your boy before you have their consent, it's going to backfire on you. First, make sure that they're ready, and then start their training. This way, they will throw no tantrums or grow fussy about going to the potty. They have to be interested, they have to be willing to try it, and they must be physically capable of going to the potty before their training can begin.

Tip #2

Girls: They Wanna Have Fun

Talking to your girl in a candid, friendly, and exciting manner about their toilet training, and explaining every step in an affirming manner will go a long way in them being receptive to their training. Make it fun, make it exciting; make it memorable.

Boys: Squatting First, Standing Second

It's not etched in stone or anything, but it's better if you teach your boy to sit down first to pee and poop, and then learn how to stand up and pee later.

Tip #3

Girls: Looking Cute Will Get You Results

Girls are extremely interested in buying colorful underwear for themselves. Use that as an incentive to train them by taking them out underwear shopping. Pick out the ones they like the most, and make them wear them when they're at home. Who doesn't like buying fresh, new, exciting underwear?

6. Boys: Let Them be Pants-Free

There's no shame in letting your boy roam around the house, not wearing any pants. If they're doing that of their own volition, let them. If you want to quicken the process, do it yourself. Take off their pants and their diapers and just leave them with their shirt on. When they have to go, they'll let you know, and you can take them to the potty. If they make a mess, at least they won't dirty their pants or use any diapers. So, win/win situation, right?

Tip #4

Girls: Treating Them to Some Sweets

Girls will be more receptive to sweet treats than boys because boys are more likely to be immersed in some activity while going on their potty as compared to girls. So, what incentive should girls be offered in place of immersion? The answer is simple. Sweets. Mini

M&Ms are the best sort of treats to give them after every successful potty run. You can give them one for when they go number one, two for when they go number two, and three if they wipe properly. Think of it as sweetening the deal for them. Do you remember that your parents used to give you treats when you went to the potty as a child? If you do, think of the positive effect this will have on her long-term memory when she recalls this as an adult.

Boys: They Want to Have Some Fun as Well

For boys, the entire process of potty-training should be a fun-centric one, as it appeals to their nature. For girls, this isn't as big of an issue. But for boys, you will have to make sure that their peripheral interest is captivated by the book, a song, a movie on their tablet, or a toy that they like. At first, it shall be just a source of distraction, but down the road, it will become a sort of a stimulus to go and use the potty more often. And that's what we want, right?

Tip #5

Girls: The Importance of Wiping

As we have discussed before, this is not a problem for boys as much as it is for girls. Boys can wipe either way, and that's fine, as long as they're cleaning themselves up properly. For girls, you must teach them the correct way to wipe. Do you remember what that is from the previous sections of the book? That's right: from the front to the back; this is crucial to feminine health! Girls have an opening to their most precious organs, and if teach them to wipe back to front, they will be bringing up germs and bacteria to that opening, causing urinary tract infections, which can be both very painful are very irritating. They're hell to get rid of, considering the age of the child.

Boys: Focusing on Getting it Done

For boys, try to get their potty-training done as quickly as possible once you have begun. This is because dragging it on for weeks or even months will not help them or you. Your boy will lose interest if the process takes too long, showing this by way of throwing a tantrum or getting irritated when they have to go to the bathroom. Besides, think of it from your perspective: you will get sidetracked by all the things going in your own life. This will eventually lead to frustration on both ends, and we don't want that. Just stay consistent, wrap it up as conveniently and quickly as you can, and you'll see the benefits of it in both your lives.

Tip #6
Girls: What Does Going to the Bathroom Entail?

Kids, and specifically girls, are very literal in terms of interpreting your commands. When you tell your girl to go to the bathroom, what exactly does she understand from that phrase? Does it mean that she'll go inside the bathroom and come out without doing anything? Of course not, but she may not understand that. You have to give her step-by-step instructions to go to the bathroom, use the potty, and then wash her hands. Trust her in that she'll understand it as long as you have explained it very simply and clearly.

Boys: Make Them Comfortable First

Comfort is a big issue for boys, as unlike girls, they have dangly bits in terms of private parts. The diaper or the underwear might be causing them suffocation down there, what with everything packed so tightly that it debilitates their movement. If you notice that that's the case, buy them new underwear and choose diapers that are a size larger.

Another way you can make things comfortable for him is by checking to see if he's using the potty easily. Some potties, although they're generically the ideal size for your child, do not sit well with your son. He might want a bigger or a comfier potty, preferably with a bigger bowl and handles. If they're feeling uncomfortable still, it might be better to skip the potty altogether and put them on the grown-up toilet with a child seat on top.

Tip #7
Girls: Do-It-Yourself Toilets

Girls, by their nature, want things to be clean, tidy, sparkly, and, well, how do I put it, girly. A do-it-yourself potty is a perfect opportunity to get their interest aroused in potty-training. Take her shopping with you and buy a DIY potty kit that she likes. Take it home with her and help her assemble it, put glitters and stickers on it, and let her become familiar with it. If she treats it like she treats her doll-house or dolls, she will become devoted to it and spend more time on it. It's simple child psychology at play here.

Boy: Don't Make Them Bored

Today's parents notice an interesting difference between boys and girls, often stating that boys are more likely to want to have fun, and girls want to be cleaner – in general. This translates to potty-training, as well. Your boy is easily distracted by distractions in their immediate environment, such as their videogames, toys, books, etc. If they get bored by sitting on the potty, they're not going to want to repeat the dreadful ritual. Instill their interest by adding their favorite games into the mix, so the potty-training time is associated with fun and excitement rather than boredom. Boys aren't as concerned with making a mess as girls are. Boys will look at it as a matter-of-fact thing they did and move on. Girls are likelier not to want to make a mess.

Tip #8
Girls: Let Them Know You're Proud

Letting your baby girl know that mama and dada are proud of her for going to the bathroom is not only going to serve as a well-needed ego boost for her self-esteem but remind her that she's doing something right. What's that, you ask? That's her going to the bathroom successfully. By giving your girl her love and adoration, you'll be setting her up to go to the bathroom more favorably than before, since she wants to become a grownup fast. This is because of the physiological and mental development difference between boys and girls, making girls mature faster, and thus wanting to appear older faster than boys.

16. Boys: An Alarm Clock Will Do Wonders

And we don't mean an actual alarm clock. It's you who must turn into their alarm clock, alerting them that they have to go to the bathroom. That's because boys are more energetic by nature, and they constantly run around, playing, screaming, experimenting, interacting, and experiencing new things all the time. In this time, if they have a diaper on them, they'll go in it, and boom, back to playing. But if they don't have a diaper on, they'll make a mess, and we don't want that. So, pick a duration of time beforehand, and remind your son to go to the bathroom at each interval, telling them they can play later once they're done with their pooping and peeing. We'll discuss this in more detail in the next chapter, i.e., Forming Potty Habits.

Tip #9

Girls: Ditching their Diapers

By their nature. girls want to appear older than they are when they're little. Call it the big girl effect, call it mimicking, whatever suits you – it's a fact! There's a reason the colloquialism "boys will be boys" is so popular; it's because boys are prone to staying juvenile longer than girls. So, when it comes to ditching diapers, it will be different for your girl. Here you have swap her diapers for underwear altogether, stressing that now they are a big girl and that diapers are for little girls. Their minds will be able to comprehend and implement it faster than you think.

Boys: Introduce a Little Competition in the Mix

Boys are competitive by nature. Use this to your advantage. Add competition to the mix by giving them something to aim at the toilet. While we previously discussed dyes and Cheetos, try to add something a little different. Maybe colorful biodegradable rings that are easy to flush? How about cereal? Tell them to aim their pee at the cereal and hit every single one of them. When they feel that they're pitted in a battle of wits against cereal, they'll make sure to come out on the other side, victorious.

Tip #10

Girls: Acquaint Them with Your Potty-Time

Although your little girl is growing up quickly and adapting to everything that you're teaching her, it might do her training well if you helped her by way of showing instead of telling. Hey, it works in writing fiction, it can very well translate to potty-training and work here too. You can take them to the bathroom with you and demonstrate the way that you go about going number one, going number two, and how you wipe yourself. Also, when your daughter sees that other members of the family are also using the toilet, it will automatically click in her head that it's something grown-ups do, and her desire to become a grown-up herself will catalyze the training process.

Boys: Time for their Big-Boy Underwear

As we previously discussed, getting big-girl underpants for your girl is going to have an enormous impact on how she sees potty-training. Well, it holds true for boys. Time to take them out on a trip to their favorite clothing store and to pick out some underpants that they like. Normally, the selection will include action heroes, trains, or something that they are specifically interested in, so let their imaginations run wild; let them choose the ones they want. Be aware beforehand, they are going to favor the superhero underpants! It might be Batman's logo that they want to cover their tooshie or Spiderman's webbed underwear. You can help them pick out several underwear that will make them excited for their training, as they'll get to see their underwear more and more whenever they take their clothes off and when they are sitting on the potty. Makes sense, right?

Chapter Nine: Forming Potty Habits

Potty-training isn't just a discrete task. It comes with peripheral habits that are necessary to teach your toddler. Some of these essential potty habits include:

Managing Paper-Waste

Toilet paper waste management should be taught to the toddler from day one. Whether it's them who's doing the wiping or you are doing it for them, teach them that the toilet paper is *not* something that you should throw away in the trash bin. Rather, it's something that should be flushed away. Make them understand that it's smelly, that it's bad, that it must not be touched from the dirty end, that it should be gotten rid of right after they or you are done using it, *and that the only proper way to get rid of it is by flushing it.* After showing them how to flush it once or twice, you should let them throw it in the toilet and flush it themselves to form the habit.

Flushing

Whether you're teaching them how to flush their used toilet paper or the contents of their potty, getting your child to flush the toilet is another important habit that should be taught early on. If your toilet has a lever, you can make a fun game out of it called "pull the lever." If it's a button, it can get a little tricky, as most buttons are a little harder to push for toddlers. If that's the case, then you should assist them by pressing the button with them. If that's impossible, at least have them accompany you when you flush the toilet, so they know that that's part of the potty process.

Washing Up

Okay, so washing their hands is another essential part of their potty-training and a very vital habit of picking up on early on. Right after they've gone potty their first time, you should introduce them to the concept of soaping their hands up, turning the tap on, lathering, rinsing, and cleaning their hands under the flow of water, turning the tap off, and drying their hands on a towel. Sometimes, children get scared of all the routine. In that case, break it down into a series of steps that you can teach them one by one. First, just have them become familiarized with the sink. You can put up a stool in front of the sink – and should have a kiddie stool that is both colorful and sturdy. Distract them by showing them their reflection on the mirror above the sink. Then acquaint them with the faucet. There are a variety of children-friendly soaps available in the market, soaps that make a lot of bubbles, soaps that are very fragrant, and soaps that are very colorful. Pick any of those to make the washing up routine more cheerful and playful for them. You can add a variety of toddler-friendly towels too.

Taking Aim

Girls won't have this issue as they'll have to pee sitting down. Boys must be taught how to pee standing up. This is a habit that will form over a week or a couple of weeks. It will create a mess for the first few days, during which they won't be able to control their stream. You can teach them to hold their penis and direct their stream at the water in the bowl. If they're not getting the hang of it (pun intended), you can train them to sit down and pee for the first few days and try again once they're comfortable with peeing while sitting.

Emptying the Toilet

After they are finished using the potty, tell them that their waste needs to go in the toilet and needs to be flushed. For the first few weeks, you'll likely be doing this yourself. But after the second or third week, they should be able to empty the potty on their own and be able to flush the contents. However, this is a very temporary habit, as they won't always be using the potty. In the next chapter, we shall be covering the transition from potty to the adult toilet. If this feels too tedious of a habit for your toddler, you can skip it.

Putting Their Clothes Back On

With boys, they might want to roam around naked in the house. This might be fine for a few days, but this cannot go on forever, can it? They need to be taught how to put their clothes back on. Are they able to pull their clothes off before going on the potty? If they're able to do that, then they're also able to put their clothes back on after they're done. You're going to have to assist them for a week for that before they're able to do that one their own.

Informing a Parent/Caregiver They Have to Go

Before they're completely independent, your child has to inform an adult they need to go. Cultivate this habit early in their training to avoid messes. If you're available, they should be able to tell you they have to go. If a caregiver such as a nanny or a grandparent is available, they should be able to tell them that. The easiest way to get them to do that is by being frank and candid with the child. The child will only confide in the person they are comfortable with. They'll turn away from the person who scolds and reprimands them. And we've already covered how punishments and scolding are very counterintuitive and have no place in potty-training.

The average time it takes for a person to form a habit is 21 days. Do you want to form your child's potty-going habit? Why not try the

21-day technique? It's neither too long nor too short. Just 21 days sounds manageable, right?

Let's break the process down into a 21-day plan that you can easily follow. We'll cover the first eight days of the 21 days. You can repeat the routine described below for the rest of the 13 days.

1. This is the most important day for their potty-training. Choose Saturday as the starting point so that you're not busy, and so you have the whole weekend ahead to give all your attention to the habit-forming routine. On this day, wake up as early as you can and wake up your toddler half an hour after you have woken up. The half-hour window is for you to get ready, go to the bathroom, get some breakfast. Once you've done all that, wake your toddler up and check his or her diaper. What do you see? Is it just pee, or is there poop inside it too? If there's poop too, it might not be the right time to get them off diapers. Consider that for later in the routine. If it's just pee, is the pee warm or cold? If it's cold, it means that they recently wet it in their sleep. If it's warm, or better yet, dry, it means that they can stay dry for longer than two hours in their sleep. This is good; this is progress.

Now take your child to the potty and have them go at it. If they go naturally, that's good. If they don't, consider putting them on the potty later in the day; once they are done, put their diaper back on. Throughout the rest of the day, you have to keep checking their diaper at every two-hour interval to see if they're staying dry or not. Half the training comprises of getting them out of their diapers. So, the first 11 days of the training will be concerned with weaning them off of diapers. How is your child responding to their first day of potty-training? If they're responding well, it's a good sign, and it bodes well for the rest of the 20 days. In the evening, after dinner, limit their liquid intake and see how they respond to that. Take them to the potty about every two hours. If you haven't started a chart for yourself, make one. These days there are a ton of apps that come with pre-made charts for your potty-training routine, so take advantage of the easiest app you can find. It's even better than written charts because that way, you get reminders in the form of chimes and alerts on your phone. At the end of the day, have them go to the potty one last time, then put their diaper on, and tuck them in their bed.

2. The second day, Sunday will involve you doing the same things as Saturday, except now might be a time to have a one-on-one talk with your toddler about their training. Using simple, toddler-comprehendible terms, tell them about what you two did yesterday and how that's important and should be continued for the next 19, 20 days. Make them aware of their potty-training.

You can reward them for understanding this. Now, again with the two-hour intervals, keep a check on their diaper dryness.

3. Make sure you're sticking to the routine by constantly checking the charts and assist them if they need assistance in going to the potty. You can ease them in by playing with them, keeping them occupied, and rewarding them every second or third attempt on the potty. Try to keep an eye out for them pooping or peeing elsewhere if they are avoiding the potty. Repeat the nighttime routine by tucking them in the bed after making them use the potty and putting a fresh diaper on them.

4. Now, this is a tricky day, as it's a Monday, the most dreaded of all days. If you're a parent with a job, it means you have to leave your baby with a caregiver or a daycare. Before, daycares often try to hasten the process of potty-training, thereby botching it and causing emotional and mental scarring to the child. If you can find a suitable daycare that guarantees that they don't rush the process, that's better. But you should confirm it by observing them potty-train your child once or twice, just to be sure. You can ask your toddler about the potty-training at daycare once they're home with you. If their expressions and words suggest confusion and fear, the daycare is doing them more harm than good.

Caregivers, on the other hand, include nannies and relatives such as grannies, are an excellent resource because they have trained other kids before, and they're going to give your kid the personal attention they need. Before you head into work, take note of your child's diaper's dryness and wetness and jot it down in your chart. Keeping note of everything is key here. That's why we recommended getting an app in the beginning. If you're more of a journaling person, always keep a diary at hand. It's for your convenience, as it will point out a pattern to you after the first week has passed, the pattern being of their toileting times, their consistency, the nature of their stool and pee, and when they wet their diapers during sleep and when they stay dry.

5. Day four gets a little easier as you move on to Tuesday. Repeat the same routine as before, being mindful of the charts, being aware of your child's behavior, and discussing their potty-training with the daycare or the caregiver. If you're on the job, notice that your lack of presence affects the child differently. Supplement for the time lost by playing with them, attending them when they call for you, and being a bit more immersed in their potty-training routine during the hours you're home.

6. You are in the middle of the week, the worst two days have come and gone, and now you can relax a bit and notice how your relaxation is emulated in your child. It's likely (and at least hopeful) that they have picked on their training, they are more receptive to it, and they are inclined on their own to use the potty. But you should not ditch their diapers just yet. For that, we must arrive at day seven.

7. On Thursday, take your toddler out and splurge on some underwear that they like. Pick out at least three to four of them so that you have an easy time cleaning them when or if they make a mess in them. These underwear are for their diaper ditching process. Once back home, carry on with the two-hour routine as usual. You'll start noticing that their diapers stay dry for longer than two hours now. This is because they are adapting to the training.

Please note that if at any step of the training you feel like they are regressing, stop the training for a few days. If the progress is uniform and consistent, keep on keeping on. If you were offering rewards every day to your child for successful potty-runs, consider dialing them back down, as too many rewards tend to spoil your child and create a Pavlovian effect.

8. TGIF! It's likely that you don't have to work tomorrow (and you deserve that break!) You've got the entire weekend to yourself and your child, and you can devote this time to the next step of your potty-training, i.e., diaper ditching. Goodbye, diapers, we do not need for you anymore. Today you should closely observe your child's diapers - more rigorously than any other preceding day. If things go as planned, they are close to not needing them any longer.

If they're keeping dry for over three hours, it's time to save a ton of money on diapers. Replace those diapers with the underwear you bought!

Notice how excited your child gets when they wear their new underwear and notice how eagerly they use the potty. Since now they're not going to be wearing diapers at night, you should be more vigilant about their nighttime liquid consumption and taking them to the potty before they sleep.

Expect accidents to happen. Prepare for them by wet-proofing their bed, as discussed in the nighttime training section.

9. We're back on Saturday. You can relax into your weekend routine by waking up at a normal time, treating yourself to some breakfast, and enjoying a well-deserved break from your parenting for about a good half-hour. Often, we, as the parents, forget to take care of ourselves while we're focusing on our child. Our self-care is equally important. Go check your child's bed. If the bed is dry and if they're sleeping soundly, you can let them sleep a little longer and maybe catch up with some friends on the phone, read a book, watch something on Netflix, or hang out with your partner. Are

there any chores around the house that need doing that are impossible to get done with your baby around? Make use of this time and some chores.

Wake your toddler up later than usual, take them to the bathroom and have them use the potty. Remember that they're not always going to poop or pee in the potty, but you still have to take them so the habit forms and becomes concrete.

Since today is their first day without diapers, observe their behavior as they go about their day. What are they doing? Are they feeling more liberated without their diapers, or do they look confused and scared? If it's the latter, hold off reverting to the diapers for a day or two. The confusion and fear are only temporary and will ease away once they become more accustomed to the potty. If it doesn't go away after more than a day, and if more accidents involving them pooping and peeing in the house occur, revert them to the diapers momentarily. But since we're taken seven whole days to taper off their diapers, the likelihood of something like that happening is little.

We have discussed a whole week of potty-training. By this time, your child should have a rudimentary grasp of their potty-training process. If they become autonomous after one week, that's all for the better. But if it feels like they need more time, repeat the instructions for week two, and then week three, letting them become more and more autonomous and independent with the progression of each week. That'll be 21 days in total. By the end of those 21 days, your child's habit will have firmly formed, and many accidents will have minimized to being nonexistent. In the end, consult all your notes that you kept in your journal or app and see the progress. Has it been steady or exponential? What went right? What went wrong? Note these down for your next child or for advice to give to another parent.

The only step left is to transition your child from their potty to an adult toilet.

Chapter Ten: From Potty to Adult Toilet

First of all, congratulations on making it to the final chapter of this book. This right here is progress. Now let's address the last stretch, the final hurdle—transitioning from the potty to the adult toilet. After this, there are no more milestones in the potty-training journey to achieve. Let's quickly review what we have done so far. We've gotten your child to ditch their diaper, we've set up their daytime routine on the potty, we've formed their habit, we've formed their nighttime routine, we've covered some basic do's and don'ts, busted some myths, and tackled some potty related problems. All that remains now is how to shift your child from a potty to the toilet.

Presently, the biggest issue you will face is your child's preference for the smaller potty. They are not to blame here, as, in the previous section, we formed their habit of going on the small potty over 21 days. Now they are accustomed to it. The transition can get tricky, just as the transition from diaper to potty was tricky. But you have to stick to the mantra: this too shall pass. It's only natural to ask yourself how long this phase will last. If only there were a concrete number of days to tell you; sorry, that's never the case.

Your inner sleuth might be doing some detective work by checking up on their pooping and peeing patterns, noticing a break you can utilize and introduce them to the grown-up toilet.

You might have noticed something else. While initially, the appeal of the potty was way too high compared to the diapers, now, on the other hand, after having washed and cleaned the potty for almost a month, you've grown tired of it and cannot wait to get rid of it. And the porcelain toilet is right there, just a few feet away. It's almost tempting to put your toddler on it and tell them to go on it. But that's not how you should do it. It can result in you de-establishing all the training process that you so painstakingly undertook.

When will my child stop using the small potty? That's the biggest question in your mind right now, and rightly so, so here's the answer: It all depends on your child, as with all other steps of potty-training. Consider the fact that a month ago, they were still in their diapers, attuned to pooping and peeing while they were standing up, sitting down, lying down, without a worry, without sticking to any schedule. Then, all of a sudden, they were plunged into a regimen where they were forced to sit down on an alien plastic potty, a seat with a hole, and they had to release their pee or poop. Remember, that was quite a bit for them to take in – sometimes, a little too much for them. They barely had any time to acquaint themselves with the plastic potty, and now you're expecting them to make such a huge developmental leap. As with transitioning from diapers to potty, a child will transition from potty to the porcelain toilet at their own pace.

What makes a child potty-trained? Well, if they have less than two pee-related accidents in a single week and no poop-related accidents, a child is considered potty-trained. Is your child potty-trained after their 21-day potty-training regimen?

If so, let's consider their age. What age-bracket are they in? A child at the age of 22 months will have difficulty in maintaining their balance on a regular toilet without the assistance of a toilet seat. They'll also need a stepstool to get up on the toilet. If your toddler's size is too small, they're going to find the toilet too high and scary to sit on.

If that's the case, keep them on the potty and wait for them to grow up a little in size before putting them on the toilet again. There's no rushing this part of the potty-training. It's the last leg of the training. If your child is getting their poop and their pee in the potty, they're doing what you taught them to do, and that's what matters, isn't it? It's not the vessel that matters as much as what they're trained to do.

Bugging your child about it won't do them any good. It'll only make them feel insufficient and lower their self-esteem.

Did you know that pooping and peeing in a squatting position is easier for your child than in a sitting position? It's also more beneficial, health-wise. That's why it's better to let them stick to the potty for a little while longer.

Another crucial factor is the dropdown. Your child has been pooping in the diaper for years. The sensation of pooping in the diapers versus the sensation of pooping in the potty is entirely different. Now add the feeling of pooping in a toilet in the mix. It's another completely alien feeling, one with drop down added. First, let your child get acquainted with using the potty, i.e., with dropping their poop down, then move on to the bigger toilet. This part of the transition should be as gradual as possible.

The Right Age to Transition to the Toilet

The average age at which a child is completely potty trained is 36 months, which, incidentally, is also the age at which they can easily transition to an adult-sized toilet. At three years of age, a child starts going to a preschool or starts spending time at the homes of other kids their age, so using a toilet becomes necessary, as potties won't always be available for them at these places. So, as their parent, you should get them acquainted with using a full-sized toilet at that age. At that age, their bodies are ready, as are their minds. This task will be almost as difficult as getting them to use the potty. You might need to resolve some emotional issues to get them to use the toilet. Fear, for example. Hesitation, anxiety, apprehension, resistance, and familiarity with the potty.

To ease them with the toilet, you can put their potty right next to the toilet. This will familiarize the child with the toilet whenever they use the potty. The next step involves you buying a toilet seat for your child. Add a stool for their feet support. After they have made the shift to the toilet, remove the potty altogether.

Tips to Make the Transition Easier

1. Post-it Notes for Public Bathrooms

Public bathrooms have self-flushing mechanisms that can sometimes scare your child when they auto-flush. To stop them from doing that, you can take post-it notes and put them on the sensors so that they don't flush when your child's poop or pee drops in the bowl. When they are done going, you can remove the post-it note, and the toilet will resume flushing. Simple, yet genius, right?

2. Headphones for Public Bathrooms

Noise-canceling headphones for public bathrooms work wonders for kids who are anxious about the loud noises in public spaces. The loud noises of people, hand-drying machines, doors opening and closing, and traffic can put performance pressure on a child, making it difficult for them to go. By putting noise-canceling headphones on their head and playing their favorite music on it, you can help them alleviate their anxiety, making it easier for them to go to the bathroom.

3. Teaching Them Toilet-Paper Etiquette

Now that they're able to use the toilet on their own, they should be taught basic toilet-paper etiquette. This includes taking two sheets, breaking them off, folding them, placing them on their butt, wiping them twice, folding them again, wiping them again, then disposing of them again in the toilet bowl. This isn't exactly a discrete habit, as it comes under the domain of going to the bathroom. You can teach this to them in tandem with teaching them to go on the potty.

4. Reading Toilet-Training Books with Them

There's an abundance of children-oriented potty-training literature available on Kindle and in paperbacks that you can read with your child as you help them transition from the potty to the toilet. This will both serve to distract them and inform them of their progress.

5. Cleaning Up After Them

Especially after your boys. After your son has started going to the toilet, they'll start observing their elder brothers, their father, their uncles, and other men at the public bathrooms use the toilets and the urinals standing up. They'll want to use it standing up as well. Besides, you'll have trained him to stand up to pee. They will make a mess the first few times when they're using the toilet, but once they've gotten command over their stream, the mess will take care of itself.

6. Decorating their Bathroom

Even though you've helped in this important transition, the fact remains that they're still a child. If their bathroom is decorated colorfully (with their favorite vibrant shades), they're more likely to spend more time in there. But don't go overboard with the decorations, or they may want to spend ALL their time in there! They must learn that their bathroom is a special room with a special purpose.

7. Assisting Them Now and Then

While independence is a huge step for your kid, it's recommended that you keep an eye on them occasionally to see if everything's going okay and if they need any assistance. Sometimes they'll need you to assist them at a public place where they'll be facing potty-resistance, such as a daycare or a public bathroom.

8. Switch the Parents

We've got a confession to make. We were saving the best advice for last. It's this: If you are having a tough time training your toddler, try switching the parent. If you're a mom, try passing on the responsibility baton to daddy, and if you're dad, try handing over the task to mommy dearest. It can make a remarkable difference when these roles are reversed, regardless of where you are at in the potty-training process.

Conclusion

Now that we've covered all the possible theoretical bases about potty-training, where do you go from here? Well, onwards, you go into that great battlefield known as parenting, armed with the weapon of this profound knowledge, onwards unto the breach! Just kidding. You can relax. Much of this information might have felt a lot to take in, especially if you are a first-time parent. Remember that not all of it is applicable all the time. You have to keep applying it day-to-day.

Let's summarize what we learned in a short paragraph, shall we?

First, we learned what the right time to start potty-training is. In this section, we focused on toddler habits, their growth, and the signs that indicated that your child is ready to begin learning how to use the potty. In the next chapter, we debunked some potty-training myths and misconceptions. Further on, we learned how to ditch diapers without the drama. Then we learned the psychology of potty-pooping and how a botched training can lead to negative effects that can last a lifetime. After that, we guided you through using the potty for the first time and how to assist a child if necessary. Then we elaborated on some potty and pooping problems, some minor accidents, the child's stubbornness, their fears, and ways to solve and prevent problems. We discussed the nighttime potty-training method after that, in which we answered questions, such as whether the child should or shouldn't be woken up at night. There's a difference between potty-training girls and boys. We discussed that in an entire chapter. In the second-last chapter, we discussed how to form potty habits and a few other habits that should complement their main habit. Last, we discussed how to transition your child from their potty to the full-grown toilet.

Equipped with this knowledge, you're now able to potty-train your child properly and carefully. We wish you the best of luck!

Resources

10 Positive Parenting Solutions to Deal with Toddler Tantrums. (2017, July 31). Kids Club Child Care Centres website: https://www.kidsclubchildcare.com.au/parenting-solutions-for-toddler-tempers/

Advice for Sleep Training Your Toddler. (n.d.). Happiest Baby website: https://www.happiestbaby.com/blogs/toddler/toddler-sleep-training

Barakat, I. (2017, March 10). Positive Discipline and Child Guidance | Living Montessori. Living Montessori Education Community website: https://www.livingmontessori.com/positive-discipline-and-child-guidance/

Bellefonds, C. (2018, December 4). Nightmare or Night Terror? What to Expect website: https://www.whattoexpect.com/toddler/sleep/toddler-nightmares-night-terrors/

Bilich, K. (n.d.). 12 Common Potty-Training Problems. Parents website: https://www.parents.com/toddlers-preschoolers/potty-training/problems/12-common-potty-training-problems/

Bhandarkar, S. (2013, November 18). Positive Discipline 101: How to Discipline a Child in a Way That Actually Works. A Fine Parent website: https://afineparent.com/be-positive/positive-discipline.html

Brill, A. (2017, November 17). How to correct a child's 'bad' behavior with positive parenting. Motherly website:

https://www.mother.ly/child/practicing-positive-discipline-with-your-kids-is-not-only-possible-its-powerful

Eisenberg, N., Zhou, Q., Spinrad, T. L., Valiente, C., Fabes, R. A., & Liew, J. (2005). Relations among positive parenting, children's effortful control, and externalizing problems: a three-wave longitudinal study. Child Development, 76(5), 1055–1071. https://doi.org/10.1111/j.1467-8624.2005.00897.x

Gagne, C. (2019, November 2). How to stop co-sleeping: An age-by-age guide. www.todaysparent.com website: https://www.todaysparent.com/family/family-health/how-to-stop-co-sleeping-an-age-by-age-guide/

Godfrey, D. (2019, July 25). Bedtime Without Struggling. Positive Parenting website: https://www.positiveparenting.com/bedtime-without-struggling/

How to correct a child's 'bad' behavior with positive parenting. (2017, November 17). Retrieved from Motherly website: https://www.mother.ly/child/practicing-positive-discipline-with-your-kids-is-not-only-possible-its-powerful

How to Potty Train: The Guide to Positive Potty Practices. (n.d.). www.kindercare.com website: https://www.kindercare.com/content-hub/articles/2015/january/toilet-training-the-guide-to-positive-potty-practices

Jones, A. (2019, June 21). 12 Positive Parenting Techniques To Make Potty Training A Peaceful Event. Romper website: https://www.romper.com/p/12-positive-parenting-techniques-for-potty-training-according-to-experts-18020415

Li, P. (2016, December 17). Positive Parenting - 8 Tips to Discipline The Happy Way. Parenting For Brain website: https://www.parentingforbrain.com/what-is-positive-parenting/

MONTESSORI AT HOME: Positive Discipline Examples & What To Do [YouTube Video]. (2019). https://www.youtube.com/watch?v=SckUevGH-Pk

Neppl, T. K., Conger, R. D., Scaramella, L. V., & Ontai, L. L. (2009). Intergenerational continuity in parenting behavior:

mediating pathways and child effects. Developmental psychology, 45(5), 1241–1256. https://doi.org/10.1037/a0014850

Novak, S. (2018, June 27). Potty Training Tips. What to Expect website: https://www.whattoexpect.com/toddler/potty-training/how-to-start-potty-training/

Phillips, R. (n.d.). Toddlers 101: Understanding Toddler Development. Parents website: https://www.parents.com/toddlers-preschoolers/development/behavioral/toddlers-101-understanding-toddler-development/

Tantrums at All Ages: What is normal? (2020, February 19). Positive Parenting Solutions website: https://www.positiveparentingsolutions.com/parenting/tantrums-at-all-ages

Toddlers and Challenging Behavior: Why They Do It and How to Respond. (2019). ZERO TO THREE website: https://www.zerotothree.org/resources/326-toddlers-and-challenging-behavior-why-they-do-it-and-how-to-respond

Tired Mom Supermom - Providing Support On Positive Parenting. (n.d.). Tired Mom Supermom website: https://tiredmomsupermom.com/

Toddler Development. (2019). Medlineplus.gov website: https://medlineplus.gov/toddlerdevelopment.html

www.ingramcontent.com/pod-product-compliance
Lightning Source LLC
Chambersburg PA
CBHW070046230426
43661CB00005B/781